PERSUASIVE WRITING SKILLS AND ACTIVITIES

Paragraph Structure	PW 1
Organizing Notes I	PW 2
Organizing Notes II	PW 3
Audience /Purpose I	PW 4
Audience/Purpose II	PW 5
Audience/Purpose III	PW 6
Writing Introductions I	PW 7
Writing Introductions II	PW 8
Supporting Your Opinion I	PW 9
Supporting Your Opinion II	PW 10
Developing Your Reasons I	PW 11
Developing Your Reasons II	PW 12
Writing Conclusions I	PW 13
Writing Conclusions II	PW 14
Revising I: Mechanics	PW 15
Revising II: Editing	PW 16
Revising III: Word Choice	PW 17
Writing Sentences I: Combining	PW 18
Writing Sentences II: More Combining	PW 19
Writing Sentences III: Fragments and Run-ons	PW 20
Sentence Variety I	PW 21
Sentence Variety II	PW 22
Details Unrelated to Topic	PW 23
Redundancy (Repeating Ideas)	PW 24
Pro/Con Approach I	PW 25
Pro/Con Approach II	PW 26
Problem/Solution Approach I	PW 27
Problem/Solution Approach II	PW 28
Persuasive Writing: Countering Technique I	PW 29
Persuasive Writing: Countering Technique II	PW 30
Persuasive Writing: Countering Technique III	PW 31
Practice and Review I	PW 32
Practice and Review II	PW 33
Practice and Review III	PW 34
Practice and Review IV	PW 35
Practice and Review V	PW 36
Practice and Review VI	PW 37
Practice and Review VII	PW 38
Persuasive Writing: Outline Form	PW 39
Persuasive Writing Topics	PW 40
Persuasive Writing: Signal Words	PW 41

Name _____

Date _____

PARAGRAPH STRUCTURE

Information: A good paragraph is well-organized and discusses only one topic or idea. A good paragraph has three basic parts:

1. an introductory statement
2. a series of sentences to support the introductory statement
3. a concluding statement

Directions: Read the following paragraph and respond to the questions and directions that follow it.

There is no doubt that the Lions are the best football team in the league this year. In the first place, they have the most explosive offense in the league. Their average of 36 points per game proves this. Also, the Lions' defense is outstanding. It has allowed fewer yards per game rushing than any other team in the league and has given up only eight touchdowns in twelve games. Furthermore, when the score is close and the end is near, the Lions always deliver that clutch play to win the game. In conclusion, if the evidence presented above does not convince you that the Lions are the best in the league, then let their 12-0 record speak for itself.

1. What is this person's opinion? _____

2. How many reasons does the author give to support the opinion? _____
_____

3. How does the author prove that the Lions' defense is good? _____
_____

4. What is the introductory statement? _____

5. What is the concluding statement? _____

6. Which sentences support the introductory statement? _____
_____
_____
_____
_____

7. Is this opinion convincing? _____ Why? _____
_____
_____

PW 1

Name _____

Date _____

ORGANIZING NOTES I

Situation: The principal of your school has given you an opportunity to express your opinion about changing the present lunch program to a "fast-food" operation. Check one of the following two choices:

1. I favor a "fast-food" lunch program. _____
2. I favor the present cafeteria program. _____

Directions: The following is a list of some ideas for and against the "fast-food" lunch program. Below the list, organize these notes into two columns. Feel free to add any ideas of your own that are not listed.

---

less expensive

better service

more nutritious

wastes (more or less) paper products

pays attention to students' likes and dislikes

tastes better

no wasted food

better variety

For Fast-Food Program	For Present Cafeteria Program

In the columns above, the ideas are listed in a random order that is hard to follow. Ideas must be organized into some order before writing. After they see their ideas organized, some people might even change their opinion. Did you change yours?

1. I favor a "fast-food" lunch program. _____
2. I favor the present cafeteria program. _____

Assignment: Using the notes you organized, write the final draft of your paragraph on the school lunch program.

PW 2

Name _____

Date _____

ORGANIZING NOTES II

Directions: Read the situation and write the reasons *for* and *against* the issue.

Situation: In a recent questionnaire your U.S. Representative to Congress asked you to respond to the following question: "Should the military draft for both men and women over 18 years of age be enacted into law by the U.S. government?"

Reasons For	Reasons Against

Information: Writing out the reasons behind each side of an issue may help you:

1. Decide which side of an issue you support.
2. Express clearly your reasons for taking one side or the other.
3. Understand better what your opponent's arguments will be.

Assignment: Write the first draft of your position on this issue using the reasons you organized on the chart above.

Name _____

Date _____

AUDIENCE/PURPOSE I

Information: When writing a persuasive essay to convince someone else of your opinion, it is extremely important to remember to whom you are writing. Are you trying to convince your parents, a teacher, the principal, a board of education member, or a friend? That individual or group is your *audience*. Why are you writing to them? The reason for your writing is the *purpose*.

Directions: Listed below are three situations for which you may write a persuasive essay. After reading each situation, indicate the audience and purpose.

1. You have recently received your driver's license and would like to purchase a used car. Although there is enough money in your savings account, your parents are likely to say "no" to the request. Try to persuade them of your point of view. Give at least two reasons for your position with examples or details to support each reason.

   Audience _____

   Purpose _____

2. Because of an increase in burglaries and vandalism, the local city council is considering a weekday curfew of 9:30 p.m. for anyone under 18 years of age. The council has asked teenagers for their opinions on this issue before they make a decision. State your opinion on the curfew and give at least two reasons for your position with examples or details to support each reason.

   Audience _____

   Purpose _____

3. The new principal of your school has asked the students to identify the problems that exist in the building and to suggest how these problems might be corrected or improved. Describe to the principal two problems you have noticed in your school and give as many specific ways as you can think of to correct them.

   Audience _____

   Purpose _____

Assignment: Choose one of the three situations and write a well-organized, persuasive essay.

Name _____

Date _____

AUDIENCE/PURPOSE II

Information: The same message may be written in several different ways, depending on the *audience*. Are you writing to a friend, a teacher, a school board member, or a legislator? Your selection of words, your tone, and even your reasons could be drastically different when writing to these different audiences.

Directions: Read the two paragraphs and answer the questions that follow.

Paragraph A

I believe the proposal to change the legal driving age from sixteen to eighteen years of age in our state is impractical and would prove very costly to implement. First, there are currently 148 students in our school who are registered to drive cars to school. Multiplying that number by all the other schools in the state would mean that thousands of students would be required to seek alternative transportation. Is the state government prepared to pay the cost of all the new school buses that would be needed to transport these students? Second, many teenagers in this bracket have full- or part-time jobs and need to drive back and forth to work. Also, many families—especially those living in rural and suburban areas—rely on their older teenagers to help with necessary chores requiring transportation, such as shopping. In conclusion, sir, I urge you to reject this proposal because it is impractical and is likely to be very expensive to carry out.

Paragraph B

As the educational leaders in our community, I hope you are aware of the reasons why the proposal to change the legal driving age from sixteen to eighteen is unrealistic. Almost 150 students now drive to school in cars, and many of them participate in the work-study program you adopted two years ago. Very few of these students could continue in the program without their own means of transportation. Also consider the many students who participate in extracurricular activities like band, dramatics, and athletics. How would they get to and from school at odd hours? In addition, imagine what would happen if 150 more students decided to ride the buses to school tomorrow morning. I think you understand the problems that would be caused—especially to the taxpayers! For the reasons stated above, I urge you to contact our state legislator and encourage him to reject this proposal.

1. Who is the audience in Paragraph A? _____

   In Paragraph B? _____

2. What is the purpose of Paragraph A? _____

   Of Paragraph B? _____

Assignment: The editor of your local newspaper agrees with the proposal to raise the legal driving age. Write this person a persuasive paragraph trying to change his or her mind. You may want to use the same reasons given above, or examples different from those given in the paragraphs.

PW 5

Name _____

Date _____

AUDIENCE/PURPOSE III

Situation: Because of declining enrollments and increased costs, there is a possibility that several boys' and girls' sports, including tennis, golf, and softball, will be dropped next year. In addition, courses in art and industrial arts may also be cut.

Directions: Select two of the audiences listed below and write a persuasive paragraph to each. In each paragraph give at least two reasons why you support or reject either of the cuts in the school program. Support your reasons with good examples or details. Try to write each paragraph differently, using a different tone, a different selection of words, and different reasons.

1. friend
2. principal
3. superintendent of schools
4. board of education member
5. parents
6. athletic director

Paragraph 1

Audience _____

Purpose _____

_____
_____
_____
_____
_____
_____

Paragraph 2

Audience _____

Purpose _____

_____
_____
_____
_____
_____
_____

Name _____

Date _____

WRITING INTRODUCTIONS I

Information: You have learned that there are three basic parts to a well-written paragraph. For some people, it helps to use one of the phrases listed below when writing the paragraph's introductory statement. Can you add any others to the list?

From my point of view ...
In my opinion ...
It is my belief that ...
I question whether ...
I disagree that ...
I maintain that ...
There is no doubt that ...

Directions: Three topics are listed below. After thinking about each one, write an introductory statement for each. You may use any of the phrases above or any other phrases you can think of in writing the statements.

1. cheating _____

_____

_____

_____

2. physical fitness _____

_____

_____

_____

3. going steady _____

_____

_____

_____

Assignment: Write a short paragraph on one of the topics. First organize your notes both *for* and *against* the topic. Then begin the paragraph by stating your opinion in the introductory statement. Complete the paragraph by giving at least two reasons to support your opinion.

Name _____

Date _____

WRITING INTRODUCTIONS II

Directions: Read the following situation, questions and sample answers, and sample introduction.

Situation: The junior class has $1,400 in its treasury. The class officers have invited you and all other members of the class to submit suggestions for using the money in your senior year. Each student has been asked to state what he or she would do with the money and to give at least two reasons why the idea is a good one.

<u>Questions and Sample Answers</u>

1. Who is the audience? *The class officers*

2. What is the purpose? *To suggest how the class will spend its money*

3. What is your opinion? *We should use the money to help pay for a senior class trip to Washington, D.C.*

4. What are your reasons? a. *educational*
                        b. *entertaining*
                        c. *memory not soon forgotten*

<u>Sample Introduction</u>

In my opinion, our class should use the $1,400 in our treasury to help finance a senior trip to Washington, D.C. during our spring vacation. Let me explain why I think this trip would be very educational, entertaining, and memorable.

Assignment: Reread the situation, then write your own answers to the questions and write your own introduction. Finally, complete the paragraph(s) explaining the reasons for your opinion.

PW 8

Name _____

Date _____

SUPPORTING YOUR OPINION I

Information: Anybody can state an opinion, but not everyone is able to convince someone else with solid reasons or examples *why* his opinion is a good one.

After writing and_____?_____your notes, you should then write your_____?_____. After writing this opinion, support it with convincing reasons or examples.

It is often helpful to use one of the words or phrases in the box below to let the reader know exactly what and where your reasons are.

first	furthermore	equally important
in the first place	also	in addition
second	moreover	likewise
third, etc.	again	similarly
next	besides	finally
further	last	

Directions: Read the paragraph below. It does not use any of the linking phrases or words listed in the box. Answer the questions that follow the paragraph.

> In my opinion, the school cafeteria should offer a salad bar as well as the hot lunch counter already available. The present hot lunches are very starchy and fattening. Some students would probably waste less food because they would only serve themselves what they really like. Salad lunches don't give you that slow, heavy feeling that makes it difficult to work in the afternoon. When students are served tray lunches they only eat what they like, so they probably don't get a very balanced meal. For the reasons above, you can understand why I feel a salad bar should be offered as part of our cafeteria menu.

How many reasons are given to support the opinion that a salad bar should be offered? _____ Where do each of these reasons begin? _____

Write the first two words of each sentence that is a reason supporting the opinion. _____

_____

_____

_____

Assignment: Rewrite the paragraph using a linking phrase at the beginning of each sentence that gives a reason supporting the opinion.

PW 9

Name _____

Date _____

SUPPORTING YOUR OPINION II

Information: It is sometimes hard to think of ideas that will help you support or reject an issue. If you could remember a few key words that relate to almost any issue, you might be able to get started.

Directions: Study the list of "trigger words" in the box below. Then read the situation and write an opinion statement. Choose three of the trigger words and write how you might use these words to support your opinion.

Trigger Words

money	safety	friendship	education	responsibility
time	energy	equality	environment	transportation
health	danger	pleasure	cooperation	conservation

Situation: Your friend, who attends college in a city 65 miles from your home, has invited you to attend Spring Weekend. Other than going away to camp for two weeks, you have never been away from home without your parents or other family members present. You are not sure how your parents will react. Therefore, you have decided to write for their permission to go.

1. Opinion statement _____

_____

2. Trigger word #1 _____ How will this support your reason?

_____

_____

3. Trigger word #2 _____ How will this support your reason?

_____

_____

4. Trigger word #3 _____ How will this support your reason?

_____

_____

Assignment: Write the paragraph to your parents using the four points described above to support your opinion.

Name _____

Date _____

DEVELOPING YOUR REASONS I

Information: It is sometimes not convincing enough to just give a reason that supports your opinion. It may be necessary to go into detail about each reason so that the reader knows exactly what you mean.

Directions: Read the following paragraphs and decide which one is more convincing.

Paragraph A

Snowmobiles are dangerous to operate and destructive to property. First of all, many snowmobile drivers haven't had the necessary experience and some have not even learned the safety regulations. You can see why there were three deaths and over 35 accidents related to snowmobiles in our county last year. Snowmobiles can also destroy property. Last year the county sheriff received more than 20 complaints about damage to fruit tree orchards and wheat fields caused by snowmobiles. In addition, many fences were knocked down. As I have said, snowmobiles are both dangerous and destructive.

Paragraph B

Snowmobiles are dangerous to operate and destructive to property. First of all, many snowmobile drivers don't know how to operate them. They just buy them and then drive them. Second, many of these drivers have never learned the rules and regulations. Finally, snowmobiles damage property belonging to others. People who ride on them and damage property don't respect other people's property. To sum up, snowmobiles are dangerous to operate and destructive to other people's property.

Which paragraph is more convincing? _____ Why? _____

_____

_____

Sometimes you need more information about each reason in order to make your argument a stronger one. Try to think of any examples, facts, figures, or any other details that prove your reason.

Assignment: Select a topic from the choices below and write a paragraph about it. First you will write any _____ you can think of. Next you will _____ those notes. Then you will write your _____.

        1. Teenagers are lazy   2. Homework is a waste of time

Remember: Use examples, details, and facts to support your reasons.

PW 11

Name _____

Date _____

DEVELOPING YOUR REASONS II

Information: When developing a reason for your opinion, how many facts, examples, or details will you use to support it? If you expand the examples or details beyond three sentences, then it is best to present another reason in a separate paragraph.

How do you develop a reason? By asking certain questions (When? Where? Who? What? What happens? How? What kind of?) it is easy to expand the reason.

Directions: Read part of the opinion statement and the questions and paragraph that follow.

"Snowmobiles are dangerous to operate"

<u>When?</u> when people are inexperienced; when conditions are poor
<u>Where?</u> in unfamiliar areas; away from marked trails
<u>Who or What?</u> those who haven't learned safety rules
<u>What kind of?</u> foolish; poorly maintained snowmobiles
<u>Why?</u> because some are careless or don't think; some drive too fast
<u>What happens?</u> accidents; injuries; deaths

Snowmobiles are dangerous to operate. This is especially true when they are driven by inexperienced or untrained people who have not learned the safety regulations. They are also dangerous when weather conditions are poor and when people drive them off trails or in areas with which they are unfamiliar. It is a known fact that many accidents occur because operators drive too fast or owners do not properly maintain their vehicles. You can understand, therefore, why there were three deaths and more than 35 accidents related to snowmobiles in our county last year.

Assignment: You have just read an example of how an opinion statement can be expanded into a paragraph by answering several basic questions. Read the following opinion statement and write answers to the same questions. Then write those answers in paragraph form.

"Snowmobiles are destructive to property."

When? _____

Where? _____

Who or What? _____

What kind of? _____

Why? _____

What happens? _____

PW 12

Name _____

Date _____

WRITING CONCLUSIONS I

Information: It has been said that every successful movie has a powerful ending. A strong paragraph also has a powerful ending, or *conclusion*. At first, your conclusion might just be a repetition of the introduction. As you improve in your writing, however, your conclusion may summarize the whole paragraph. You might even offer some kind of solution in the conclusion.

Just as some people like to use an introductory phrase before their introduction, others like to use a concluding phrase before their conclusion. Look at the list of these words or phrases in the box below. Be sure to use a comma after any of the concluding phrases listed.

for the reasons given above	in summation
for the preceding reasons	in conclusion
as you can see	in other words
in sum	as I have noted above
to sum up	without a doubt
in brief	in any case
on the whole	in the final analysis
in short	in any event

Directions: Read the paragraph below and write a conclusion for it. Use a concluding phrase to get started if you need it. Compare yours with those of others in the class.

The most exciting form of entertainment for me is watching a horse race at a racetrack. My excitement starts to build while I watch the horses warm up before each race. It mounts as the horses approach the starting gate and the crowd hushes, directing its attention to the starting bell. As the race begins, I am almost bursting with the thrill of the competition. My eyes are glued to the horses as they round the track for the final stretch. I feel a shout of joy or a groan of disappointment escaping me as the horses cross the finish line.

_____

_____

_____

_____

PW 13

Name _____

Date _____

WRITING CONCLUSIONS II

Information: You know that a conclusion can be merely a restatement of the introduction. Sometimes, however, it is necessary to expand that restatement into a separate paragraph. How do you expand a conclusion? Read the questions and answers below and notice how the questions have been answered in the sample conclusion.

1. Have you repeated your opinion? This is a must.

2. Did you use a signal word or phrase? It helps.

3. Who is your audience? It is polite to mention the name(s).

4. What are your reasons? Include the key words from each in your conclusion.

5. Can you offer another solution to the problem? Think of one.

Sample Conclusion

(2) As you can see, (3) Mr. Silver, your proposal to cancel our field trip to the United Nations and New York City (1) is questionable. If you did this, you would not only (4) be punishing the whole class for the foolish acts of a few, but also (4) be denying an educational and cultural opportunity of a lifetime to the majority of us responsible seniors. Why not consider an alternative solution, such as (5) providing early transportation home for those who misbehave?

Directions: Read the following situation. List your opinion, at least two reasons or examples for that opinion, and any details that support the reasons or examples. Finally, write a conclusion by answering as many of the five questions above as possible.

Situation: In your school there have been several thefts from lockers and empty classrooms during class periods. Mr. Howard, the assistant principal, has notified all teachers that students may no longer leave class or study hall during class periods, except for emergencies. Write to Mr. Howard expressing your opinion about his decision.

Name _____

Date _____

REVISING I: MECHANICS

Information: When you write the first draft of an essay, you are more interested in organizing your thoughts and information in sentences and paragraphs than in things such as spelling. It is only natural to make errors in spelling, capitalization, punctuation, and grammar. It is important to read through your rough drafts carefully looking for any errors. Many people also read them orally to see if they "sound" right.

Directions: Read the paragraph below and look for any mechanical errors.

I prefer to live in the Country rather than the City for several reasons. Their is less air pollution in the Country. Because there is fewer cars and factories to spew poisonous hydrocarbons into the air. Living in the Country better for you're health. Also, Country living is superior because of the extra available to grow fresh fruits, vegetables and flowers. Furthermore everyone know there is a lower crime rate in the city. Their will be less chance of someone hurting you. I guess you can understand why I prefer to live in the Country.

Check any problem areas found in the paragraph.

_____ spelling   _____ punctuation

_____ grammar   _____ words omitted

_____ capitalization   _____ other

Assignment: By yourself or with a small group, revise and rewrite the paragraph to eliminate the mechanical errors.

PW 15

Name _____

Date _____

REVISING II: EDITING

Information: Most writers are well aware of the need to make revisions in their rough drafts in the areas of spelling, punctuation, capitalization, and word usage. However, it is also important to check for other problems. Sometimes we put words or phrases in the wrong place, repeat ideas, forget to write an introduction or conclusion, include unrelated information, or even write in a disorganized way.

Directions: Read the paragraph below and look for any editorial errors.

Year-round school calendars should be adopted in our state beginning next year. When we close our schools for long periods of extended time, we are wasting space. When we waste space, we also at the same time waste money. My cousin goes to a year-round school in Florida, but he dislikes it. Why spend thousands of dollars on expensive buildings when we don't use them 75-80 days in the whole year? When we send students home for long vacations, they usually get bored after the first ten days anyway. Schools should be open year-round with short, ten-day vacations in between ten weeks of classes when it will be more better to operate next year when inflation soars even higher.

Check any problem areas found in the paragraph.

_____ organization   _____ repetition of ideas

_____ words out of place   _____ conclusion

_____ unrelated information _____ other

_____ introduction

Assignment: Revise and rewrite the paragraph to eliminate the editorial errors.

REVISING III: WORD CHOICE

Information: When you write a first draft you are most interested in getting the ideas and information on paper. Therefore, you do not always think of the best word or phrase at that time. Sometimes you put a word or phrase in the wrong place. Other times you use a word or phrase too often. While reading through your first draft, you may decide to replace a word or phrase with a more precise word.

Directions: Read the paragraphs below and circle any words or phrases that are overused, cross out any unnecessary words, and underline any words that can be expressed more precisely.

Some people think "camping out" means going to an electrified campsite in their $10,000 travel trailers. They have all the comforts of home, including soft beds, bathrooms, and heaters or air conditioners. They have all the camping supplies to cook outdoors, but instead they have to go to the store to buy prepared foods to cook in the travel trailer. They even have refrigerators, stoves, and television sets.

I think camping means going to an outside area where you can pitch a tent and cook a meal on an open fire, without hearing a television or radio blaring. I think camping means walking to an area where animals roam free and talk to each other. I think it means sleeping on the ground in a tent. In conclusion, camping should be a getaway from home, not a home away from home.

The paragraphs above have many characteristics of an excellent essay. They are well-organized and have no errors in mechanics. However, repetition of words and poor word selection have weakened the message.

Assignment: Rewrite the paragraphs using more accurate and varied words.

Name _____

Date _____

WRITING SENTENCES I: COMBINING

Directions: Read the following paragraph.

There is more to do with your spare time in the city than in the country. You can go to a big-league game. You can sometimes visit a museum, a zoo, or a park. I like going to the movies. There are many movies from which you can choose in a big city. People live closer together there than they do in the country. There are more kids to do things with. It is easy to travel around for all these activities in the city. The public transportation is excellent. I really believe that the city offers much more to do with your spare time.

Check any problem areas found in the paragraph.

_____ poor punctuation   _____ organization

_____ no introduction   _____ too choppy

_____ no conclusion   _____ opinion not supported

_____ nothing wrong

Information: There is a problem with the paragraph. Although there are no obvious mistakes, the paragraph reads choppily. All of the sentences are short, with a simple subject and a simple predicate. Why not try to combine some of the ideas into longer sentences? The paragraph will read better when you do.

Assignment: Use the connecting words in the box below to rewrite the paragraph. When you are done, compare your sentences with those of others in the class.

or	because
and	but
therefore	for
yet	so

PW 18

Name _____

Date _____

WRITING SENTENCES II: MORE COMBINING

Information: You have learned that simple sentences can be combined into longer, more complicated sentences by using certain connecting words such as *but, or, for, and, so, therefore, nor,* and *yet.*
There are additional connecting words that you can use to combine simple sentences. These are listed in the box below.

though	before	when	as long as
if	as	while	whenever
as if	as soon as	because	due to
although	since	because of	even though
after	until	unless	in order to

Directions: These connecting words can be used in either the first part of the sentence or the last part of the sentence. Read the examples:

1. Jim had an accident. The party was over.
   Jim had an accident <u>after</u> the party was over.

   OR

   <u>After</u> the party was over, Jim had an accident.

2. Her car did start. She decided to walk.
   <u>Even though</u> her car did start, she decided to walk.

   OR

   She decided to walk <u>even though</u> her car did start.

Assignment: Using the connecting words listed above, combine the following sentences in two different ways, as shown above.

1. Frank will be the boss. John returns to work.
2. My vegetables were destroyed. We had temperatures below freezing.
3. I could not concentrate on the speech. People were whispering to each other all around me.
4. You set up the tent behind the barn. I will make sure the owner gives us permission.

PW 19

Name _____

Date _____

WRITING SENTENCES III: FRAGMENTS AND RUN-ONS

Information: Two frequent errors in writing are sentence fragments and run-on sentences. What are they? Look at the examples below.

Fragments	Sentences
(Don't express complete thoughts)	(Do express complete thoughts)
1. When the boys left home.	1. When the boys left home, I was very lonely.
2. All the girls in the chorus.	2. I felt sorry for all the girls in the chorus.
3. Hansel and Gretel lost their way. While watching for some birds.	3. Hansel and Gretel lost their way while watching for some birds.

Run-On Sentences	Proper Sentences
1. Venus is a planet we are studying in school it is many miles away.	1. Venus is a planet we are studying in school. It is many miles away.
2. The police were called they sped to the scene of the accident.	2. The police were called and they sped to the scene of the accident.
3. The reading was very difficult, the assignment impossible.	3. The reading was very difficult, so the assignment was impossible.

Directions: Read the following paragraph. Try to identify any sentence fragments and run-on sentences.

Collecting antiques is an enjoyable and profitable hobby for a growing number of people today. Many people who are seriously interested in history. Collect everything from books to buttons. These kinds of items give us direct contact with the ideas and customs of past generations. That they represent. Other people get pleasure from collecting old furniture, it is often more useful and better built than modern furniture. In addition, there are some people who collect anything old. When they hear about some antiques selling for hundreds or thousands of dollars, they look for *any* item that might bring them a windfall. In short, more and more people are collecting antiques for fun and profit.

Assignment: With a small group, discuss some of the problems found in the paragraph and think of different ways these problems could be corrected. Rewrite the paragraph correcting any sentence fragments and run-on sentences.

Name _____

Date _____

SENTENCE VARIETY I

Information: Some people write paragraphs consisting mainly of simple sentences. Others use mostly compound or complex sentences. An excellent way to improve your writing style would be to use a variety of sentence types in your paragraphs.

Directions: Read and compare Paragraphs A and B. Then answer the questions that follow.

Paragraph A

The sun is our best energy resource of the future. First, our supplies of natural gas, oil, and coal are not endless. However, it seems our supply of solar energy would be sufficient for eons. Nuclear energy could be used for centuries, but we are all aware of the dangers of radioactivity and waste products. Another source of energy is electricity, yet we need coal or oil to produce it. In conclusion, the best part about solar energy is that we don't have to produce it. We only have to learn how to harness the abundant supply of it.

Paragraph B

The sun is our best energy resource of the future. Our supplies of natural gas, oil, and coal are not endless. Nuclear energy could be used for a long time. There are dangerous waste products and radiation involved in the production of nuclear energy. Electricity is a clean fuel. Plants need either coal or oil to manufacture it. We don't have to make solar power. The sun has an abundant supply of it. We could use it forever.

1. How are Paragraphs A and B similar? _____

2. How are Paragraphs A and B different? _____

3. Which do you think is the better of the two? _____ Why? _____

_____

_____

Assignment: Discuss your answers with a small group of other students in your class. Then present your group's answers to the rest of the class.

Name _____

Date _____

SENTENCE VARIETY II

Directions: One way to check for sentence variety is to count the number of words per sentence. Another way is to check the sentence patterns. Read the paragraph below and answer the questions that follow.

Swimming is an activity that provides the best exercise for most people. Constant movement of arms, legs, and trunk make it a total body exercise. Most of the body's muscles are therefore working at the same time. Swimming is different from other types of exercises like running and bicycling. It does not jar the bones or cause damage to knees and ankles. Also, it seldom stretches or pulls muscles, cartilage, or tendons. I think swimming is the best total exercise for people of all ages.

1. How many sentences are in the paragraph? _____ Count the number of words per sentence and list here:

   _____
   _____
   _____

2. Could you improve the variety of sentences by changing the length of sentences in a paragraph? _____
   Why or why not? _____
   _____
   _____
   _____

3. What sentence pattern (subject/predicate; predicate/subject) is used in each sentence? _____
   _____
   _____
   _____
   _____

4. Could you improve the paragraph by changing the sentence patterns? Why or why not? _____
   _____
   _____
   _____

Assignment: Rewrite the paragraph. Use a variety of sentence patterns, including signal words, and vary sentence lengths.

Name _____

Date _____

DETAILS UNRELATED TO TOPIC

Directions: Read the following paragraph. Try to identify any problems that may be present.

Our sources of energy are rapidly decreasing, yet we are so wasteful. In the first place, some people drive their cars unnecessarily and without any purpose. Second, supplies of natural gas are so scarce in some states that schools and factories must close during part of the winter months. At the same time, people in other states refuse to help by turning down their thermostats. A friend of my brother has a fireplace, but he doesn't even use it. How many people do you know who waste energy by playing the television too long or leaving the lights on when they aren't needed? Also, we should stop buying oil from foreign countries because we will become too dependent on them. Finally, because the world's population is increasing so rapidly, we need to conserve our present supplies for the future.

Check any problem areas found in the paragraph. Be ready to support your answer.

_____ introductory statement   _____ sentence variety

_____ mechanics (spelling, grammar, etc.) _____ details not related to topic

_____ concluding statement   _____ word choice

Assignment: Look at the topics listed below. Each has a list of possible details that might support the introductory statement. However, some of the details are *unrelated* to the topic. Put an X on the line next to these unrelated details. Then write a paragraph on one of the topics.

Fiction is my favorite kind of reading material.	Of all seasons, summer is the most entertaining.	Teenagers should earn their own spending money.
___ characters like Paul Bunyan and Pecos Bill ___ biographies of famous Americans ___ poems are fun, too ___ events not real, but it's interesting to pretend ___ songs are poems put to music	___ stay around the house ___ picnic in the park ___ swim at the lake ___ wait for school to close for holidays ___ play ball with friends	___ some kids don't know math ___ will help keep kids busy and out of trouble ___ parents need free time ___ teaches how to handle money ___ my brother and sister have jobs

PW 23

Name _____

Date _____

REDUNDANCY (REPEATING IDEAS)

Directions: Read the following paragraph. Try to identify any problems that may be present.

The cafeteria service and menu at our school is really outstanding. The workers are always courteous and helpful when we file through the line. Although some students do not exactly use the best of manners, the cafeteria staff is always helpful and polite. Most days the menu is both nutritious and tasty. My favorite is pizza day, even though I could eat more than the small slice they give us. There always seems to be a balance of the four food groups in each day's meal and those meals are usually delicious. Furthermore, the meals are nutritious and good tasting, especially the salad and pizza they serve on Friday. In summary, I believe our cafeteria staff prepares excellent meals and serves them with the skill of true professionals.

Check any problem areas found in the paragraph. Be ready to support your answer.

_____ introductory statement	_____ mechanics	_____ organization
_____ concluding statement	_____ word choice	_____ sentence variety
_____ redundancy	_____ details not related to topic	_____ other

Information: You have probably noticed that two ideas were repeated in the paragraph. How do you prevent this common problem in students' writing? Two suggestions are given below that may help to eliminate redundancy.

1. Organize your ideas or notes *before* you begin to write. In this way, you can see how many *different* ideas you have.

2. Proofread your first draft carefully, looking for any ideas that are the same. Even though you may have used different words, you may still be repeating the same idea.

Assignment: Revise and rewrite the paragraph. Make any improvements you feel are necessary.

PW 24

Name _____

Date _____

PRO/CON APPROACH I

Information: When discussing a controversial issue, there is usually a clear choice: either you agree and support a position (pro), or you disagree and reject it (con). Using the pro/con approach, you should first identify the audience and purpose. Then list some examples or reasons and any supporting details on *both* sides of the issue. Finally, organize those notes into several paragraphs to persuade the audience to accept your opinion.

Directions: Read the situation and the notes that follow.

Situation: The Assistant Superintendent in your school system has recommended to the Board of Education that it change its current policy and require all high school students to complete eighteen credits for graduation. Currently, only sixteen credits are required. Due to a heated discussion at a recent Board meeting, the recommendation was postponed until further information could be obtained. Students have been asked to write their opinions on this issue and present them at the next meeting.

Audience _____

Purpose _____

Notes

Pro	Con
more learning will take place decreases number of study halls improves overall educational system better preparation for future	those students leaving for Occupational Education or Work Study Program will not have time requires more teachers and more money less time for special help to many students

Assignment: Using either the "pro" or "con" notes, write several paragraphs to persuade the Board of Education to accept your opinion. Be sure to:

1. State your opinion clearly.

2. Explain your reasons carefully.

3. Revise before writing the final draft.

PW 25

Name _____

Date _____

PRO/CON APPROACH II

Directions: Read the situation and identify the audience and purpose. Then list your notes (both pro and con) in the spaces provided.

Situation: Even though you are an above-average swimmer, you still feel a need to improve your skills. Therefore, you want to attend a three-week competitive swim camp this summer. Your parents are questioning this request because of the cost ($200 fee, plus daily transportation). Write to your parents explaining why you want to attend.

Audience _____

Purpose _____

Notes

Pro	Con

Assignment: Write several paragraphs to your parents stating your opinion, giving at least two reasons or examples for that opinion, and details that support those reasons. Be sure to:

1. State your opinion clearly.
2. Explain your reasons carefully.
3. Revise before writing the final draft.

PW 26

Name_____

Date_____

PROBLEM/SOLUTION APPROACH I

Information: You are sometimes asked to respond to a particular problem that has no clear-cut answer. In this case, a problem is stated and you must offer a solution to it.

Although you must still identify your audience and purpose, your notes may vary slightly from the "for/against" or "pro/con" format. You should list as many solutions to the problem as possible. Then expand two or three of those by listing specific examples and details that support your solution. Finally, select the solution that best supports your position.

Directions: Read the situation and look at the notes that follow.

Situation: The principal of your school has asked members of the student body to suggest one way in which school life could be improved. Those ideas that are clearly written and supported will be considered. Explain at least two reasons how or why your idea would improve school life.

Notes

1. Expand the intramural sports program
    a. will involve more students in athletic program, especially those not good enough for varsity sports
    b. may give some students better preparation for varsity competition
    c. may reduce the number of athletic teams, thereby saving the district money
2. Provide short-term mini-courses to students
    a. could take the place of many study halls and reduce wasted time
    b. students might teach others their hobbies or interests
    c. no credit or grades would be given

Assignment: Choose one of the two suggestions listed above—or one of your own—and expand it into several paragraphs. Be sure to:

1. State your opinion clearly.
2. Explain your reasons carefully.
3. Revise before writing the final draft.

PW 27

Name _____

Date _____

PROBLEM/SOLUTION APPROACH II

Directions: Read the situation and identify the audience and purpose. Then list your notes in the space provided.

Situation: The school district's cafeteria program operated in the red last year, showing a net loss of $23,284. Next year there will be a 15% decrease in government aid, amounting to an additional $31,759 loss to the district. There has been considerable discussion in the district about this problem and the Board of Education has asked students for their opinion on possible solutions.

Audience _____

Purpose _____

Notes

Assignment: Using your notes, write to the Board of Education stating your solution. Give at least two reasons or examples for that solution and details that support the reasons. Be sure to:

1. State your opinion clearly.
2. Explain your reasons carefully.
3. Revise before writing the final draft.

PW 28

Name _____

Date _____

PERSUASIVE WRITING: COUNTERING TECHNIQUE I

Directions: A very effective way to enhance your opinion is to counter the arguments of the opposing viewpoint. Read the statements below and answer the questions that follow.

   A. <u>I realize you</u> want me to continue my education next year. <u>However,</u> I feel the need to discontinue school and work for a year or two.

   B. <u>Even though</u> you feel Senator Adams is more experienced, <u>let me explain</u> how Mr. Burnett's background makes him a better candidate.

   C. <u>I understand you believe</u> urban renewal is the best answer to better housing and neighborhoods. <u>On the other hand,</u> have you considered how urban renovation would be a less costly and more effective solution?

1. How does the writer begin each paragraph? _____

_____

_____

2. Do you think this is an effective technique? _____ Why or why not?

_____

_____

Information: You should see from the examples above that the writer knows the opponent's position and attempts to reject the argument with a solid counter-argument. This technique informs your audience that you have already considered the reason and have decided to reject it.

Remember that in order to make your "counter" effective, you must expand the paragraph to include reasons or examples and supporting details. Otherwise, your viewpoint will be no more convincing than the one you are countering.

Assignment: Either in groups, pairs, or individually develop *one* of the examples listed above. Fully explain your position with reasons or examples and supporting details.

Name _____

Date _____

PERSUASIVE WRITING: COUNTERING TECHNIQUE II

Information: If used properly, the countering technique can be a very effective way to present your opinion on an issue. The opposing viewpoint is considered, but is quickly rejected in favor of your position. Supporting details, examples, and reasons should make your opinion very persuasive.

Directions: Read the signal words listed in the box below. They may help you when countering the arguments of the opposing viewpoint. Add to the list when you think of additional signals.

I realize you . . .	believe	but,
I understand you . . .	feel	yet,
Even though you . . .	maintain	however,
Although you . . .	want	I doubt . . .
Some people . . .	support	I question . . .
Your idea to____deserves	favor	Let me explain . . .
some merit	argue	On the other hand . . .
It may be that you . . .	state	On the contrary . . .
		Nevertheless . . .

Assignment: Read the topic ideas and audiences listed below and write three topic sentences (one or two sentences per topic) using the countering technique. An example is given.

Topic Ideas	Audiences
smoking	parent
legal voting age	teacher
military draft	another student
use of public facilities	principal
changes in school policy	board of education
homework assignment	lawmaker
testing	editor of local newspaper

Example: Congressman Johnson feels all 18-year-old men and women should be required to serve their country in the military draft. I question whether *military* service is appropriate for both men and women.

1. _____

_____

_____

2. _____

_____

_____

3. _____

_____

_____

Name _____

Date _____

PERSUASIVE WRITING: COUNTERING TECHNIQUE III

Directions: Read the situation and identify the audience and purpose. Then organize your notes for both sides of the issue.

Situation: Your parents are deciding whether or not to enforce a weekend curfew of midnight for you. They want your opinion on this matter. Decide whether you think the curfew is necessary or not.

Audience _____

Purpose _____

Notes

For	Against

Assignment: Using the countering technique and the signal words, write several paragraphs to your parents stating your opinion, giving at least two reasons or examples for that opinion, and details that support those reasons. Be sure to:

1. State your opinion clearly.
2. Counter the opposing point of view in the topic sentences.
3. Explain your reasons carefully.
4. Revise before writing the final draft.

PW 31

Name _____

Date _____

PRACTICE AND REVIEW I

Directions: Read the situation and identify the audience and purpose. Then determine whether it is a "pro/con" or a "problem/solution" type of situation. Next, organize your notes in the box.

Situation: The mayor of Blackwell is deciding whether or not to have the town sponsor monthly Saturday night dances for teenagers at the Recreation Center. She wants opinions from several groups in the community, including the teenagers who live in Blackwell. Write to the mayor expressing your opinion on this issue.

Audience _____

Purpose _____

Type of Situation _____

Notes

Assignment: Write several paragraphs to the mayor stating your opinion, giving at least two reasons or examples for that opinion, and details that support those reasons. Be sure to:

1. State your opinion clearly.
2. Explain your reasons carefully.
3. Revise before writing the final draft.

Name _____

Date _____

PRACTICE AND REVIEW II

Directions: Read the situation and identify the audience and purpose. Then determine whether it is a "pro/con" or a "problem/solution" type of situation. Next, organize your notes in the box.

Situation: Each year, your school district adds extra days to school calendar to guard against the loss of time due to weather or emergency conditions. The state requires each district to be in session a minimum of 180 days. Your school had 183 days scheduled this year, with none of the emergency days used. Write to your principal expressing your opinion on what should be done with the extra three days.

Audience _____

Purpose _____

Type of Situation _____

Notes

[ ]

Assignment: Write several paragraphs to the principal stating your opinion, giving at least two reasons or examples for that opinion, and details that support those reasons. Be sure to:

1. State your opinion clearly.
2. Explain your reasons carefully.
3. Revise before writing the final draft.

PW 33

Name _____

Date _____

PRACTICE AND REVIEW III

Directions: Read the situation and identify the audience and purpose. Then determine whether it is a "pro/con" or a "problem/solution" type of situation. Next, organize your notes in the box.

Situation: An out-of-town rock group known as "Shows Unlimited" has contacted A.J. Brocker, a local farmer. The group wants to rent his 750-acre farm for the weekend of July 4 in order to have a rock concert. Although Mr. Brocker is agreeable to this, the Town Council must decide whether or not to allow this event to take place. There is quite a bit of disagreement on this topic, both on the Council and in the community. Write to the Town Council to convince them of your opinion.

Audience _____

Purpose _____

Type of Situation _____

Notes

```



```

Assignment: Write several paragraphs to the Town Council stating your opinion, giving at least two reasons or examples for that opinion, and details that support those reasons. Be sure to:

1. State your opinion clearly.
2. Explain your reasons carefully.
3. Revise before writing the final draft.

Name_____

Date_____

PRACTICE AND REVIEW IV

Directions: Read the situation and identify the audience and purpose. Then determine whether it is a "pro/con" or a "problem/solution" type of situation. Next, organize your notes in the box.

Situation: The Town Council is concerned about the rising costs of energy and the effect of those increases on the city budget. An Energy Conservation Committee has been formed to brainstorm alternatives for reducing energy consumption. This committee, among other efforts, has contacted all city schools asking students for their ideas. As a concerned student, write to the committee expressing your opinion on what could be done.

Audience_____

Purpose_____

Type of Situation_____

Notes

[ ]

Assignment: Write several paragraphs to the committee stating your opinion, giving at least two reasons or examples for that opinion, and details that support those reasons. Be sure to:

1. State your opinion clearly.
2. Explain your reasons carefully.
3. Revise before writing the final draft.

Name _____

Date _____

PRACTICE AND REVIEW V

Directions: Read the situation and identify the audience and purpose. Then determine whether it is a "pro/con" or "problem/solution" type of situation. Next, organize your notes in the box.

Situation: Your state assemblyman has sponsored Bill No. 27004 that, if it becomes law, would prohibit the sale of nonreturnable bottles and cans in your state. The bill would require that every can or bottle be "taxed" five cents. This charge would then be returned to the consumer when the bottles or cans were returned. As a concerned consumer and state resident, let your assemblyman know how you feel about this issue.

Audience _____

Purpose _____

Type of Situation _____

Notes

Assignment: Write several paragraphs to the assemblyman stating your opinion, giving at least two reasons or examples for that opinion, and details that support those reasons. Be sure to:

1. State your opinion clearly.
2. Explain your reasons carefully.
3. Revise before writing the final draft.

PW 36

Name _____

Date _____

PRACTICE AND REVIEW VI

Directions: Read the situation and identify the audience and purpose. Then determine whether it is a "pro/con" or "problem/solution" type of situation. Next, organize your notes in the box.

Situation: Your school has recently had a rash of vandalism in vacant classrooms, lavatories, and other unsupervised areas. Although the administration has caught and punished several students, they are unable to stop all of this unexplainable destruction. They are considering very drastic action that would really punish *all* students. Therefore, they have asked the Student Council to propose solutions to the problem that might not be so drastic. As a member of the Student Council, write to the administration with your opinion on this issue.

Audience _____

Purpose _____

Type of Situation _____

Notes

[ ]

Assignment: Write several paragraphs to the administration stating your opinion, giving at least two reasons or examples for that opinion, and details that support those reasons. Be sure to:

1. State your opinion clearly.

2. Explain your reasons carefully.

3. Revise before writing the final draft.

PW 37

Name _____

Date _____

PRACTICE AND REVIEW VII

Directions: Read the situation and identify the audience and purpose. Then determine whether it is a "pro/con" or "problem/solution" type of situation. Next, organize your notes in the box.

Situation: The Metropolitan Gas and Electric Corporation has purchased property in your area specifically for the purpose of constructing a nuclear power plant. A public forum has been scheduled to discuss this issue. As a concerned citizen and resident, you intend to present your views at the meeting, which is sponsored by the city council members. Write your opinion to read at the meeting.

Audience _____

Purpose _____

Type of Situation _____

Notes

[ ]

Assignment: Write several paragraphs to present at the meeting stating your opinion, giving at least two reasons or examples for that opinion, and details that support those reasons. Be sure to:

1. State your opinion clearly.
2. Explain your reasons carefully.
3. Revise before writing the final draft.

PW 38

PERSUASIVE WRITING: OUTLINE FORM

Topic _____

Audience _____

Purpose _____

Trigger Words

money	safety	friendship	education	responsibility
time	energy	equality	environment	transportation
health	danger	pleasure	cooperation	conservation

Introductory Statement _____
_____

Opinion _____
_____

Reason #1 _____
_____

Details _____
_____
_____

Reason #2 _____
_____

Details _____
_____
_____

Reason #3 _____
_____

Details _____
_____
_____

Concluding Statement _____
_____

Conclusion _____
_____

PW 39

PERSUASIVE WRITING TOPICS

1. Watching television is a waste of time.

2. Parents do not listen to (or talk to) their children enough.

3. Girls should (or should not) be permitted to participate on boys' athletic teams.

4. The best way to forget your troubles is to _____.

5. No one should be allowed to hunt unless he or she is at least 25 years old and has completed a hunter safety course.

6. People are born good; society makes them bad.

7. How a student behaves should not affect his or her grades.

8. At age 18, all young men and women should be required to serve their country for one year.

9. A college education is not for everyone.

10. A person needs many friends in order to feel needed and part of a group.

PERSUASIVE WRITING: SIGNAL WORDS

Introductory Phrases

In my opinion	There is no doubt that	I question whether
I believe	From my point of view	I (dis)agree with
It is my belief that	It seems to me that	I maintain that

Concluding Phrases

For the reasons above	To sum up	In short	In brief
As you can see	To be sure	Undoubtedly	In any event
As I have noted	Without a doubt	In conclusion	In any case
In other words	In summation	Obviously	Concluding
On the whole	Unquestionably	Summarizing	

Supporting Opinions

First	Furthermore	Equally important	Besides	Further
Second	In addition	In the first place	Next	Again
Third	Also	Likewise	Moreover	Similarly
Finally	Last			

Introducing Details

For example	For instance	In support of this
In fact	As evidence	

Cause and Effect

Since	Caused by	In effect
Because of	This results in	Brought about
Due to	Consequently	Made possible
For this reason	Accordingly	As might be expected
Therefore	As a result of	Give rise to
If ... then	Leads to	Was responsible for

Compare and Contrast

Similarly	Likewise	As well as	Whether or not
Compared to	In the same way	Have in common	Even though
In like manner	Contrasting	All are	Rather than
On the other hand	On the contrary	The same as	Nevertheless
Although	As opposed to	Conversely	In spite of

Countering

I realize you	believe	but
I understand you	feel	yet
Even though you	maintain	however
Although you	want	I doubt
Some people	favor	I question
It may be that you	support	Let me explain
Your idea to____deserves	argue	On the other hand
some merit	state	On the contrary
		Nevertheless

PW 41

DESCRIPTIVE WRITING SKILLS AND ACTIVITIES

Structuring Paragraphs	DW 1
Writing Introductions	DW 2
Knowing Your Conclusion	DW 3
Using Adjectives	DW 4
Avoiding Vague Adjectives	DW 5
Using Action Verbs	DW 6
Using Adverbs	DW 7
Combining Sentence Fragments	DW 8
Reducing Run-On Sentences	DW 9
Using Quotation Marks	DW 10
Using Similes and Metaphors	DW 11
Appealing to the Senses I	DW 12
Appealing to the Senses II: Sight	DW 13
Appealing to the Senses III: Hearing	DW 14
Appealing to the Senses IV: Touch, Taste, and Smell	DW 15
Appealing to the Senses V: Combining Senses	DW 16
Appealing to the Senses VI: Application	DW 17
Describing a Person I	DW 18
Describing a Person II	DW 19
Organizing Paragraphs	DW 20
Organizing by Position: Prepositional Phrases	DW 21
Organizing with Time Signals	DW 22
Organizing by Cause and Effect	DW 23
Organizing Ideas by Using Details I	DW 24
Organizing Ideas by Using Details II	DW 25
Revising I: Mechanics	DW 26
Revising II: Editing	DW 27
Revising III: Word Choice	DW 28
Practice and Review I	DW 29
Practice and Review II	DW 30
Practice and Review III	DW 31
Practice and Review IV	DW 32
Practice and Review V	DW 33
Descriptive Writing: Outline Form	DW 34
Descriptive Writing: Topics	DW 35
Descriptive Writing: Signal Words	DW 36

Name _____

Date _____

STRUCTURING PARAGRAPHS

Information: A paragraph contains a group of closely related sentences, all dealing with a particular topic or idea. One sentence usually states the main idea of the paragraph. The others detail and describe whatever you want to say about it. You must remember two things about the paragraph:

1. The topic sentence must be one that makes a general statement about what will follow.
2. What follows must be directly related to that topic.

Directions: Read the following paragraph and answer the questions that follow.

My sixth-grade teacher, Miss Jackson, thought I was a troublemaker and I can only guess the reasons why. Maybe it was because I enjoyed laughing and playing practical jokes on my friends. One time I convinced a friend of mine to go to the office without Miss Jackson's knowledge. He got in trouble but never told on me. Since I was big for my age and my voice began to change, Miss Jackson probably felt I had repeated a grade or two. Therefore, I must have been a troublemaker in her eyes. I'm sure she sensed that I was not so interested in school work as I was in recess or gym because I always came to school with athletic equipment of some sort. Furthermore, a student always knows when the teacher doesn't trust him or her. Those eagle-eye stares and the pacing behind my desk were warnings enough of the distrust. I guess I'll never know the real reasons, but there's no doubt she thought I was a troublemaker.

1. What is the topic? _____

2. Is it stated clearly? _____

3. Are all of the details related to the topic? _____

4. Which details are not related to the topic? _____

Assignment: Rewrite the paragraph. Eliminate those details that are not related to the topic. Add any details that might explain why the author was labeled a troublemaker.

DW 1

Name _____

Date _____

WRITING INTRODUCTIONS

Information: The introduction of a descriptive paragraph is usually the topic sentence. Writing several different "leads" or beginnings is one way to compose a clear and effective topic statement. Simply choose the best one of those you have written.

Directions: Read the topic and the three introductions given below. Then answer the questions that follow.

Swimming Lessons

a. Since I don't like water very much, except for drinking and cleaning, I was pretty scared about attending my first swimming lessons at summer camp.

b. I was very nervous about my first swimming lessons at summer camp because my experiences with water were limited to drinking it or cleaning with it.

c. Because I had never gone swimming before, my first swimming lessons at summer camp were a frightening experience.

1. Which introduction do you like best? _____ Why? _____

_____

_____

_____

2. What do you like or dislike about the other two? _____

_____

_____

_____

_____

_____

_____

Assignment: Write three different introductions or "leads" to the topic "Household Pets" or any other topic you choose. Pick the best lead and write a descriptive paragraph about it.

DW 2

Name _____

Date _____

KNOWING YOUR CONCLUSION

Information: Did you ever start with a good idea and not know how to end it? Many writers experience this problem. Some people write and write and suddenly end their writing without warning. Others think of an ending partway through and realize it won't make sense.

Some authors decide how their idea will end *before* they begin to write. Then they plot their way from beginning to end. This is an effective technique.

Directions: Read the topics below and their possible conclusions. Then write possible endings for the other topics listed.

Topic	Possible Conclusion
1. Vacation across country.	Returned home more tired than when I left.
2. Surprise birthday party.	Found out about it, but was surprised anyway when unexpected guests arrived.
3. First impression of a person.	_____
4. Moving to a new school.	_____
5. A hike through the woods.	_____
6. A subway ride.	_____

Assignment: Select one of the topics and its conclusion. Plan how you will go from start to finish. Write a descriptive paragraph (or paragraphs) on this topic.

DW 3

Name _____

Date _____

USING ADJECTIVES

Information: It is hard to imagine writing descriptively without using adjectives. An adjective modifies, or describes, a noun or a pronoun. Notice the difference between the following sentences:

1. The bear climbed the tree looking for a beehive.
2. The huge grizzly bear climbed the maple tree looking for an abandoned beehive.

Obviously, the second sentence is far more interesting and precise in its description. Remember that the adjective would answer one of the following questions:

What kind? ... <u>hairy</u> beast, <u>pretty</u> butterfly
Which ones? ... <u>seventh</u> graders, <u>those</u> cars
How much? ... <u>three</u> pounds, <u>no</u> energy

Directions: Read the following paragraphs and fill in the blanks with descriptive adjectives. Do not use any adjective more than once.

    I'll never forget the time my friends, the Ritter twins, and I decided to camp out in the _____ Cemetery. That was one of the _____ nights of my life. Before hiking down the _____ road to the entrance, we stopped at the _____ store to fill our pockets with _____ candy and _____ soda. Throwing our supplies over first, we then climbed the _____ gate and searched for a _____ place to bed down. No sooner had we settled down to tell _____ stories than the first _____ event happened. Simultaneously the moon disappeared and a _____ wind came upon us. What had been a _____ and _____ night was now _____ and _____.

    Shortly thereafter, we heard what seemed to be a _____ accident on the road near the front entrance. But we continued reading _____ books with our flashlight and eating the treats we bought earlier. Then we heard a _____ sound, and a _____ light gradually came into focus. As it got closer, I saw Tim dart behind the large, _____ monument behind us. Paul and I bolted toward the _____ bushes to camouflage our presence. It seemed as though we were safe from this _____ sight, that is, until I saw Tim's flashlight shining directly at that _____ thing, which was slowly approaching us.

Assignment: Complete the story, using as many descriptive adjectives as possible.

DW 4

Name _____

Date _____

AVOIDING VAGUE ADJECTIVES

Information: Because people use some adjectives so often and in so many ways, we really do not have an accurate or precise idea of what they mean. For example, read the following:

1. Barb said to Sue, "Bill really is a nice guy."

What does "nice" mean? Cute? Helpful? Friendly? It's difficult to understand exactly what is meant by the word "nice."

2. Frank thinks he is pretty big.

What does the adjective "big" mean? Important? Popular? Or does it mean he is "big" in size? If it refers to his size, then why not use "huge" or "enormous" or some other word that refers to size—not to personality.

Directions: Read the sentences below and in each one replace the underlined adjective with a more exact modifier. The new word should add interest and meaning to the noun and to the whole sentence.

1. I saw a <u>fantastic</u> movie Saturday night. _____

2. We think Mr. Sullivan is a <u>neat</u> person. _____

3. If you touch an electric fence, you'll get a <u>weird</u> feeling. _____

4. Your sister cooked a <u>great</u> supper. _____

5. Betty is a <u>pretty good</u> student. _____

Compare your answers with those of other students in the class. Notice how you probably used different adjectives than they did. In using different adjectives, you may have changed the whole meaning of the sentence.

Practice: Write your own adjectives in the spaces that follow. Compare yours to those of others in the class.

1. The hermit lived a _____ life in the woods.

2. Marie was a _____ student because no one really liked her.

3. We planted two _____ pine trees in our backyard.

4. After driving his motorcycle so fast, John learned a(n) _____ lesson.

5. My cousin has a _____ treehouse in her backyard.

6. No one is more _____ than Marcia when it comes to planning a party.

Assignment: Without using vague adjectives, write a story using the introductory statement given here. Use your imagination.

"I recently saw the most bizarre animal at the Bronx Zoo. It was called a Hiccalux and I'd like to tell you about it."

DW 5

Name _____

Date _____

USING ACTION VERBS

Information: Most verbs—but not all—are words that express action. The use of action verbs helps us to write more descriptively. However some of these words are better than others because they paint a clearer picture of what we are describing. Read the sentences below. Note the underlined words and answer the questions that follow.

1. The road crew will <u>make</u> a tunnel under Mount Sienna.

2. Henry <u>said</u>, "I didn't forget to bring the forks!"

3. Joan really felt proud as she <u>went</u> home with a perfect report.

The action verbs <u>make</u>, <u>said</u>, and <u>went</u>, are examples of overworked and abused words. They could be replaced with more accurate action words. Cross out those three words in the sentences above and supply the sentences with better words.

Directions: Read Part One of the story below. Replace all underlined words with more action-packed verbs by crossing out the underlined word and writing the new word above it. When you finish, compare your answers with those of others in the class.

Backfire! Part One

I desperately wanted <u>to give</u> my brother a lesson, but <u>as it turned out</u>, I was the person who <u>got</u> the raw end of the deal. As the oldest of three boys, Richard <u>got</u> the attic for his bedroom. Steve and I always <u>said</u>, "That's not fair!" to our parents, but they never <u>gave in</u> to our demands for equality.

So, one day I <u>said</u> to myself, "I will just show him a thing or two!" I would like you to know that Richard had two bad habits that really <u>got to</u> me. First, he always <u>went</u> up and down the attic stairs like a herd of elephants. Second, he always <u>went</u> around barefoot, stinking up the room I happened to be in. Well, I <u>made</u> a plan. Off I went to the corner store that bright July afternoon to <u>get</u> some itching powder and thumbtacks.

Assignment: Conclude this story by writing Part Two. Use verbs that accurately describe the action.

DW 6

Name _____

Date _____

USING ADVERBS

Information: Like adjectives, adverbs are also describing words. However adverbs modify a verb, an adjective, or another adverb. Look at the following examples:

1. The children <u>often</u> talked <u>nervously</u> when the principal was <u>there</u>.

    "Often" and "nervously" describe the verb "talked."
    "There" modifies the linking verb "was."
    An adverb can be located before *or* after the verb it modifies.

2. The <u>brightly</u> spotted guinea fowl <u>suddenly</u> disappeared.

    "Brightly" is an adverb and modifies the adjective "spotted."
    "Suddenly" is an adverb and modifies the verb "disappeared."
    "Suddenly" could be used at the beginning of the sentence.
    "Suddenly" could be used after the verb "disappeared."

3. The frightened boy ran <u>away instantly</u>.

    "Away" is an adverb and modifies the verb "ran."
    "Instantly" is an adverb and modifies the other adverb "away."

It is necessary to use adverbs regularly if you wish to write descriptively. How do you identify an adverb? Many end with the suffix "ly." However, all of them answer one of these questions:

<u>When</u>? (now, later, then, soon) . . . arrive <u>later</u>.
<u>Where</u>? (here, there) . . . threw <u>away</u>.
<u>How</u>? (calmly, patiently, quickly) . . . agree <u>wholeheartedly</u>.
<u>How often</u>? (always, sometimes) . . . <u>never</u> lie.
<u>To what degree</u>? (very, too, really) . . . <u>extremely</u> busy.

Directions: Read the following paragraph and fill in the blanks with descriptive adverbs. Do not use any word more than once.

    The last time I visited the zoo was more than a year ago, but I can _____ remember everything I saw. Especially clear in my mind are the tigers and lions. They paced _____ around their cages _____ aware of the visitors who were watching them. The elephants also noticed our presence, because they _____ nibbled peanuts and salted crackers from our hands. _____ we watched the monkeys put on a show. Even my mother and father laughed _____ when the smallest one jumped _____ up and down, sticking his tongue out at us. By the time we arrived at the refreshment stand, our empty stomachs were growling _____. After lunch, we planned to visit many other interesting areas before the long trip home.

Assignment: Describe the remainder of the zoo visit, using descriptive adverbs whenever possible.

DW 7

Name _____

Date _____

COMBINING SENTENCE FRAGMENTS

Information: Some writers have a tendency to write short, choppy sentences. These sentences can be expanded by answering such questions as When? Where? Why? How? What kind of?

Directions: Look at the following example.

A fire destroyed the Colonial Inn.
What kind of? A raging fire destroyed the historic Colonial Inn.
Where? A raging fire destroyed the historic Colonial Inn in Waterloo.
When? A raging fire destroyed the historic Colonial Inn in Waterloo last night.
Why? or How? A raging fire destroyed the historic Colonial Inn in Waterloo last night after a bolt of lightning struck the building.

Notice how the short sentence has been expanded to include more details. If you have a whole paragraph of short, choppy sentences, you can combine several of them by using any of the signal words listed in the box.

and	but	because	if	unless
or	for	when	after	while
yet	so	since	before	until

Assignment: Read the sentences below. Notice how some words are unnecessary or repeated. Try to combine all of the information in one or two sentences by using some of the signal words from the box above.

1. The monkey was at the Los Angeles Zoo.
2. The monkey lived in a large, open area.
3. The monkey's living area was surrounded by a wire fence.
4. The monkey's trainer fed him bananas and nuts.
5. The monkey liked to show off.
6. The monkey grinned and laughed at people who stopped to watch.
7. The monkey climbed large boulders.
8. The monkey swung on bars and poles.

_____

_____

_____

_____

_____

DW 8

Name _____

Date _____

REDUCING RUN-ON SENTENCES

Information: Run-on sentences are the result of overexpansion or combining too many ideas or phrases within one sentence. How can you avoid run-on sentences? Use the five suggestions listed below.

1. <u>Read your sentences orally</u>. If you pause, hesitate, or stop at certain points, you may need to insert a comma, semicolon, or period.
2. <u>Don't overuse connecting words</u>, such as "and," "when," "and then," "but," or "because." Limit the number of connecting words in each sentence.
3. <u>Watch for a change in subjects or ideas</u>. If the subject changes in the middle of a sentence, you may have a run-on sentence.
4. <u>Count the number of words per sentence</u>. If a sentence exceeds 20 words, check it carefully. Sentences of varying length improve the readability of a paragraph.
5. <u>Eliminate any unnecessary words or phrases</u>. Cross out extra words or repeated information.

Directions: Read the paragraph below with the five suggestions listed above in mind.

When my parents left me alone for the first time, I was excited about having the whole house to myself, but after a short time the sounds of the night made me uneasy because I never really noticed them before. Were the sounds normal or was there some creature or even worse a prowling thief who was trying to get into the house? First I decided to turn on all the lights and lock all the doors and windows and then I turned up the television's volume so that an intruder would know that someone was at home at this time. Watching the Alfred Hitchcock thriller *Psycho* on the television was a mistake because it made me even more aware of creaking floors, bushes scratching against the windowpane and Dr. George, our cat, jumping around upstairs. When the phone rang I jumped about three feet off the couch. It was my mother saying to me that Dad was not feeling well and that they were leaving and that they would be home in about 30 minutes. So much for staying home alone. I was relieved.

Assignment: Rewrite the paragraph, correcting the run-on sentences and eliminating as many unnecessary words as possible.

DW 9

Name _____

Date _____

USING QUOTATION MARKS

Information: Quotation marks ("...") have several specialized uses, but usually they are used to enclose or surround the exact words someone has spoken or written. When writing dialogue in descriptive paragraphs, note the following major rules. An example is also given.

1. Use quotation marks to enclose every direct quote, whether it is complete or interrupted.
2. Both parts of an interrupted quotation are enclosed in quotation marks. The first word of the second part is *not* capitalized unless it begins a new sentence.
3. A change in speaker requires a new paragraph and a new set of quotation marks.

"May I use the car tonight?" Bill asked his father as he walked into the kitchen for dinner.
"Sure," replied Dad, "if you promise two things." Then he winked at Mom and continued. "You'll have to fill up the gas tank and agree to be home by 9 p.m."

Directions: Apply quotation marks and proper punctuation to the sentences below.

1. I deny everything you have said argued the accused shoplifter. But answered Sergeant Miller you were observed by our television camera taking those items.

2. When will you come home for Christmas vacation asked her mother. Will it be the 21st or the 22nd? I should be home the 21st replied Judy if Mr. Simpson gets here early enough I'll call you before we leave.

3. Mr. Williams said over the loudspeaker today's assembly has been postponed until further notice. In the teachers' room Miss Conable said I will now be able to give the vocabulary quiz to my third period class.

Assignment: Write a short descriptive dialogue (conversation) on one of the following topics:

1. teacher and student talking about a grade on a writing assignment.
2. David asking Sara for a date.

DW 10

Name _____

Date _____

USING SIMILES AND METAPHORS

Information: Similes and metaphors are figures of speech that help to paint a clearer picture of what you are saying. They are used quite effectively in descriptive writing. Examples of these two figures of speech are given below.

Simile expresses a comparison, using "like" or "as."

Betty looks <u>like</u> an angel in that photo. (The subject "Betty" is compared to "an angel.")

Ralph is <u>as big as</u> a bear and wrestles like one, too. (The subject "Ralph" is compared to "a bear.")

Metaphor expresses a comparison in which readers use their imagination to see the likeness.

Betty is an angel in school. (The subject "Betty" is compared to "an angel.")

On the mat, Ralph is a bear. (The subject "Ralph" is compared to "a bear.")

Directions: Read the sentences below, which contain similes and metaphors. Underline the comparison and draw an arrow to its subject.

1. After a three-day absence, Rover ate like a starved pig.

2. On the gridiron, the Lions are the top of the heap.

3. They were a mass of nerves and tension after the accident.

4. He stood as still as a mannequin in a store window.

5. High in the sky the clouds were like puffs of cannon smoke.

6. His muscles turned hard as iron and he grew resistant to pain.

7. The first frost arrived unexpectedly and now the forests wear hoods of yellow and bronze.

8. In the west, the sun flared like a burning ball.

9. Muhammed Ali always proclaimed he could "float like a butterfly and sting like a bee."

10. I never liked school; it was merely a ticket to the employment agency.

11. Watching their 60-foot schooner point into the wind, I realized why she was called "the Grand Lady" of the sea.

12. The president of our student council is a stuffed shirt.

Assignment: Write six descriptive sentences of your own, three containing a simile and three with a metaphor.

DW 11

Name _____

Date _____

APPEALING TO THE SENSES I

Information: When you write a descriptive paragraph you must first focus upon an image, which will be the topic. You can expand upon this image by using your senses to highlight the details. Hopefully, when you have finished, the reader will see, hear, taste, smell, or feel the image you chose to describe.

Directions: Read the paragraph below and answer the questions that follow.

As I walked into my English class for the first time this year, I wasn't expecting anything out of the ordinary. A few new faces in the class carried expressions of anxiety and nervousness. The others I'd seen for so many years hadn't changed at all. The odor of freshly painted walls and slippery, waxed floors indicated that the summer work crew had done its job. As usual, in Mr. Highland's room the desks and chairs were arranged in perfect rows. The chalkboards and bulletin boards were practically bare, with the exception of a new calendar and the regular assortment of mimeographed rules, regulations, and daily schedule. Just prior to the first period bell I heard whisperings that echoed my own thoughts, "Where's Mr. Highland? He's not at the board ready to squawk instructions—military style—at precisely 8:07." The low hum gradually increased in volume until 8:09 when the light scent of perfume rushed through the opening door. Silence. In walked a pretty, long-haired woman, stylishly dressed and obviously new. With a smile that caught everyone's eye, she gently said, "Good morning. My name is Miss Thompson. I've replaced the retired Mr. Highland." This might be an interesting year after all!

1. What is the topic? _____

2. How does the writer feel about the topic? _____
_____

3. To which senses does the writer appeal? _____
_____

4. Write the words or phrases from the paragraph that convey each sense impression.

Sight: _____
_____

Hearing: _____
_____

Taste: _____
_____

Touch: _____
_____

Smell: _____
_____

Assignment: Write a descriptive paragraph about your first class this year.

Name _____

Date _____

APPEALING TO THE SENSES II: SIGHT

Information: Describing is really an easy task when you use your sense of sight. You can describe objects, activities, events, or people much more accurately in this way. What is your topic's color, size, or shape? What special features does it have? Is it in motion or stationary? What can you say about its surroundings? Sometimes the topic is visible while you are writing. In most cases, however, you must rely on past experience to help you visualize the topic. Follow the two steps listed below *before* you begin writing.

1. Focus on the topic—either through memory or through observation.
2. Write down any words or phrases that describe how your topic *looks*.

Directions: Read the topic below and the visual details that follow. Think about how you would organize those details as you prepare to write a paragraph about the topic.

Huge Christmas tree in department store.

Glittering ornaments reflecting light; many sizes and shapes of wrapped presents; at least 25 feet high with flashing star at the top; silvery tinsel hanging; green felt rope connected to four heavy stands; flickering red, yellow, green, blue lights; strings of popcorn draped around; first sight upon entering front door; smiling shoppers staring.

Assignment: Write a paragraph using any of the listed details (and any others you want to add) to describe the topic.

_____
_____
_____
_____
_____
_____
_____
_____
_____
_____
_____
_____
_____
_____
_____
_____

DW 13

Name _____

Date _____

APPEALING TO THE SENSES III: HEARING

Information: Appealing to the sense of hearing also helps to paint a clear picture of your topic. Listen to or try to remember all the sounds related to the object, activity, event, or person. Are the sounds loud, soft, or rhythmic? Do they blend well together or compete with each other for your attention? Does the noise you hear come directly from the object or is it part of the background? Answering these questions will help you to describe your topic more clearly and accurately. Follow the two steps below *before* you begin writing.

1. Focus on the topic—either through memory or through observation.
2. Write down any words or phrases that describe the *sounds* of or around your topic.

Directions: Read the topic below and the details that follow. Think about how you would organize those details as you prepare to write a paragraph about the topic.

Department store during Christmas holiday season.

Television programs and stereo equipment blaring; cash registers ringing; crinkling of customers' shopping bags; clerks explaining products; holiday music playing softly through hidden speakers; teenagers testing latest electronic games with computerized voices and sirens; ringing bells; the roaring "Ho, ho, ho!" of Santa Claus; crying babies; young boys and girls squealing over games and toys they want.

Assignment: Write a paragraph using any of the listed details (and any others you want to add) to describe the topic.

Name _____

Date _____

APPEALING TO THE SENSES IV: TOUCH, TASTE, AND SMELL

Information: The senses of touch, taste, and smell appeal to the reader very effectively. We are all naturally attracted to things that evoke them, and companies who advertise their products on radio and television use this technique to their advantage. Expressions like "cold and tingling," "downy soft," and "like a breath of fresh air" are used to attract our attention and create feelings of comfort and satisfaction. Try to create your own impression by appealing to the senses of touch, taste, and smell. Follow the two steps listed below *before* you begin writing.

1. Focus on the topic—either through memory or through observation.
2. Write down any words or phrases that appeal to *touch*, *taste*, and *smell*.

Directions: Read the topic below and the details that follow. Think about how you would organize those details as you prepare to write a paragraph about the topic.

Department store during Christmas holiday season.

Fluffy down quilt; scratchy sweater; cheese and cracker samples; roasted peanuts and buttery popcorn; bayberry- and vanilla-scented candles; rolling and swaying on displayed waterbed; popular fragrances from perfume and cologne counter; over-carbonated soft drink; sizzling hot cheeseburger; greasy French fries.

Assignment: Write a paragraph using any of the listed details (and any others you want to add) to describe the topic.

Name _____

Date _____

APPEALING TO THE SENSES V: COMBINING SENSES

Information: You have learned how each of the senses of sight, hearing, taste, touch, and smell can be used individually to effectively describe your topic. In reality, it might be difficult to write a paragraph that appeals to only one sense. Therefore, you should try to use a combination of two or more.

Directions: Read the following paragraph. Note how the senses are combined to form an effective picture.

As I trotted into McGuire's Department Store to buy some Christmas gifts, I was shocked by the size and beauty of their Christmas tree. Flickering red, yellow, green, and blue lights reflected off the hundreds of glittering ornaments. From the assortment of colorfully wrapped packages at its base to the glowing star on its top, that 25-foot blue spruce was a masterpiece of decoration. I was not the only one impressed by this display. Nearly everyone stopped to stare before continuing on his or her way. The piped-in holiday music was occasionally drowned out by the blaring stereo equipment, crying babies, or the electronic games with their computerized voices and sirens. But they all created a festive mood. On my way to the Junior Miss Department, I sampled the latest fragrances at the perfume counter and rolled on the displayed waterbed. I wanted to buy a sweater for my sister, but the ones I could afford were too scratchy. Instead, I bought her a bayberry-scented candle shaped like a unicorn. As I wandered about from department to department, the smell of roasted peanuts and buttery popcorn drew me to the restaurant counter. That was a mistake. The over-carbonated soda had too much syrup and the French fries were greasy. On top of that, the sizzling cheeseburger burned the roof of my mouth. On my way out, the ringing cash registers and overstuffed shopping bags indicated that customers were in a buying mood. I suddenly realized that I had a lot more shopping to do.

Assignment: List the words in the above paragraph that appeal to the five senses.

Sight _____

_____

Hearing _____

_____

Taste _____

_____

Touch _____

_____

Smell _____

_____

DW 16

Name _____

Date _____

APPEALING TO THE SENSES VI: APPLICATION

Directions: Below are two topics that you could describe very colorfully by appealing to the senses. Select one and jot down details for each sense that could describe the scene. Then write two or three possible introductions and select the best one.

1. A busy city street corner.
2. A cafeteria in school or a restaurant.

Sight details _____

_____

Hearing details _____

_____

Touch details _____

_____

Taste details _____

_____

Smell details _____

_____

Introduction #1 _____

_____

_____

Introduction #2 _____

_____

_____

Introduction #3 _____

_____

_____

Which introduction is the best? _____

Assignment: Write a paragraph or paragraphs describing your topic in detail. Be sure to appeal to as many senses as possible.

DW 17

Name _____

Date _____

DESCRIBING A PERSON I

Information: Describing a person is far different from describing an object, event, or activity. You must try to capture both the physical features and the personality traits of an individual. Does his appearance tell you something about his personality? How does he act with other individuals, in small groups, or in large gatherings? What mannerisms make him different from others? How does he walk, talk, or dress? If done well, your description will identify the person without mentioning the name.

Directions: Read the paragraph below and answer the questions that follow.

When he walks into the room you can sense the seriousness with which he performs his job. A long nose and high cheekbones dwarf the rest of his face. Black-rimmed glasses cannot hide those dark, penetrating eyes that immediately photograph all activity in the room. Meticulously dressed in a pinstriped suit and wrinkle-free, button-down shirt, he is a perfectionist. Everything and every person has its place; order and organization are the rule. He walks and stands erect, looking much like a military officer who has arrived for inspection. With a quick glance and a forced smile, he turns and walks away. He conveys his message clearly without uttering a single word. The clicking of those spit-shined shoes echoes through the halls as he makes his way back to the principal's office.

1. What are the words that describe what he looks like? _____

_____

_____

_____

2. Which words describe his personality traits? _____

_____

_____

_____

3. How does the author feel about him? _____

_____

_____

4. Why do you think so? _____

_____

5. What is your impression of him? _____

_____

_____

_____

Name _____

Date _____

DESCRIBING A PERSON II

Information: When describing a person you must try to capture both her physical characteristics and personality traits. Describe how she acts alone or with others. What does she do with her hands, eyes, and body? What does she say and how does she say it? How does her appearance or dress relate to her personality? Answering these questions might help you describe a person more effectively.

Directions: Describe a person in your class so that others will be able to identify him or her. Follow these rules:

1. Do not tell anyone else whom you are describing.
2. Do not refer to that person as "him," "her," or by name.
3. Do not describe out-of-class behavior.

Assignment: Write the description below. Appeal to the senses and organize the description in an orderly manner, such as from head to toe or from side to side.

_____
_____
_____
_____
_____
_____
_____
_____
_____
_____
_____
_____
_____
_____
_____
_____
_____

DW 19

Name _____

Date _____

ORGANIZING PARAGRAPHS

Information: There are several ways to organize descriptive paragraphs. The details, especially in sight description, should follow a logical sequence. You may describe your scene from side to side, from near to far (or reverse), or from top to bottom (or reverse). The following list of signal words may guide you in developing this organization.

base	across	interior	upward	at a distance
bottom	below	exterior	within	to (on) the left
foot	beneath	next to	close	to (on) the right
top	center	under	against	in back of
above	middle	underneath	near	in front of
behind	peak	crest	summit	leading to
beside	halfway	up	down	far

Directions: Read the paragraph below and answer the questions that follow.

I was late for the football game, but at least my car was now running properly. As I pulled into the parking lot, I could see the scoreboard at a distance. With two minutes remaining in the second quarter, the score read "Eagles 0, Visitors 0." I guessed that I hadn't missed too much. I walked through the gate leading to the stadium. The closer I got to the playing field, the more the excitement mounted. I hurried across the end zone and noticed that the Eagles were in a position to score at the far end of the field. Looking for my friends in Section B was difficult as the bodies and faces blurred together. Suddenly there was a roar, and everyone jumped up and down in a frenzy. The Eagles had scored. I stood at the base of the stands waiting for the crowd to settle down. Finally I spotted Dick and Phil about halfway up. Their faces reflected the joy and excitement of all Eagle fans as the gun sounded, ending the first half.

1. What method of organization is used? _____

2. What words signal this method? _____

Assignment: Write a paragraph describing a scene, activity, or person. Use the signal words to help you organize the information.

DW 20

Name _____

Date _____

ORGANIZING BY POSITION: PREPOSITIONAL PHRASES

Information: One way to improve your descriptive writing is to identify the position or location of your subject as clearly as possible. You can do this by using prepositional phrases. Look at the list of prepositions in the box below.

aboard	behind	from	to
about	below	in	toward
above	beneath	into	under
across	beside	next to	underneath
against	between	of	up
along	beyond	off	upon
among	by	on	with
around	down	over	within
at	for	through	without

Directions: Read the story below, placing reasonable prepositions in the blanks. Notice that the story is much more exact when you use prepositional phrases that identify location and position.

No one had ever escaped _____ Thunder Island! Major Martin planned his escape as soon as he arrived _____ this devilish island. At first he was thrown _____ the dungeon _____ ground level. It was dank and dark as he felt his way _____ the cell he was to call home _____ the next ten years. Immediately he knew that the best way out was to tunnel _____ the stone foundation, _____ the 1,500-foot prisoner yard, and _____ the snake-infested swamp. Then he could attempt to find his way _____ the sea and freedom.

Digging _____ his fingers and a flat stone that he found _____ his bed, Major Martin managed to work his way _____ the hard-packed sand for the first 50 feet _____ his journey _____ liberty. As he moved slowly _____ the torture chamber, he could hear screaming.

Assignment: Complete this story, using prepositional phrases that accurately describe position or location.

DW 21

Name _____

Date _____

ORGANIZING WITH TIME SIGNALS

Information: A writer often uses signal words to help his readers understand how the ideas in the paragraph are related to each other in time. The words in the box below can be used to show how events are related by time order or sequence.

first	then	before ...
second	immediately	soon
next	meanwhile	before long
at the same time	thereafter	finally
later	afterwards	at last
after ...	earlier	

Notice how some of these signal words are used in the following paragraph:

The weather was very changeable today. First, the sun shone so brightly I needed sunglasses. Then gray storm clouds rolled in from the west. After lunch, lightning darted across the sky and the thunder sent my chickens running for cover. Before long, huge, cold raindrops fell in a torrent. Later that afternoon, the rain stopped, the clouds disappeared, and the blue sky finally reappeared.

As you can see, the underlined signal words help to identify the order in which things are happening. These signal words can be especially useful when writing a summary, a book report, or a story.

Assignment: Write your own story, using the introductory sentence below. Be sure to use the signal words whenever possible.

"That one day as an invisible person was really an unbelievable experience for me!"

DW 22

Name _____

Date _____

ORGANIZING BY CAUSE AND EFFECT

Information: Certain events or activities can lead to *(cause)* another event *(effect)*. You can use this cause and effect pattern very effectively when writing descriptive paragraphs. The signal words listed in the box below may help you to organize your paragraph in a cause-and-effect pattern.

since	because	thus	caused by
due to	therefore	so	as a result of
because of	consequently	if—then	for this reason
whenever	when		

Directions: Read the paragraph below. Look for the signal words or phrases that indicate when one event may cause something else to happen. Then answer the questions that follow.

It was one of those hot, sticky, stormy nights when even the soundest sleepers would be lucky to get more than three hours of sleep. A heavy vapor hung over the city like a soaked blanket; the result of a late afternoon thunder shower. The temperature registered 81° at 10 p.m., and I'm sure the humidity was 100%. Consequently, my sweat-covered body could not find a comfortable spot in which to relax, much less fall asleep. I could tell another storm was brewing when flashes of lightning in the distance disrupted the 11 o'clock radio newscast. I must have fallen asleep for a short time when all at once a crack of thunder shook my apartment and caused me to sit up in bed instantly. I could hear the gusts of wind and driving rain beating against my window. As I lay sleeplessly on my bed, it seemed the storm would never end. Suddenly I realized it was daylight, and my heart jumped when I looked at the clock. It read 2:59. Obviously the storm had caused a power blackout. Racing around the apartment, I hoped I would not be late for work.

1. List the words or phrases that signal causes or effects in this paragraph.

_____
_____
_____

2. What are some of the causes and effects used in this paragraph? _____

_____
_____
_____

Assignment: Choose one of the three topics listed below or one of your own and write a descriptive paragraph using the cause-and-effect pattern of organization. Use the signal words when necessary.

1. A traffic accident you observed.
2. An argument between two students.
3. A party you attended.

DW 23

Name _____

Date _____

ORGANIZING IDEAS BY USING DETAILS I

Information: One way to organize ideas in descriptive writing is to brainstorm for words or phrases that come to mind when you think of a particular topic. Then organize those random thoughts according to a plan. You could describe your topic from outside to inside, from top to bottom, from one spot to another, or from far to near. Remember to start your paragraphs with a general statement about the topic.

Directions: Read the topic below and the details that follow. Think about how you would organize those details as you prepare to write a paragraph about the topic.

An old barn in the country.

Weather-worn; dull red with faded white letters advertising Mail Pouch Tobacco; haven for field mice and farm cats; pigeons perched on huge 12-inch beams; burdocks and grape vines crawling up sides; standing idle for many years; alongside country road; notice every time I drive by; old stone foundation crumbling; door blown off; rough to the touch; could see daylight through holes in the siding and roof.

Assignment: Write a paragraph using the details listed above (and any others you want to add). Remember to organize the ideas according to a plan and to write a good topic sentence.

_____
_____
_____
_____
_____
_____
_____
_____
_____
_____
_____
_____
_____
_____
_____
_____
_____
_____

Name _____

Date _____

ORGANIZING IDEAS BY USING DETAILS II

Directions: Choose one of the following topics and try to visualize or imagine in detail what it looks like, sounds like, smells like, or even feels like. What does it remind you of? What can you compare it to? How do you feel about it? Write down these thoughts quickly; they do not have to be in any particular order. Then decide how you will organize the details.

Topics

1. Christmas or birthday morning.
2. a burned-out building.
3. a messy bedroom.
4. your first day of school.
5. a county or state fair.
6. your choice of any other topic.

Details

_____
_____
_____
_____
_____
_____
_____
_____
_____
_____
_____
_____
_____

How will you organize these details? _____

_____

Assignment: Write a descriptive paragraph using the details listed above. Remember to organize the ideas according to a plan and to write a good topic sentence.

DW 25

Name _____

Date _____

REVISING I: MECHANICS

Information: When you write the first draft of your descriptive paragraph, you are probably interested primarily in organizing the details into sentences and paragraphs. It is only natural to make errors in spelling, capitalization, punctuation, grammar, and usage. It is important to read through these first drafts carefully looking for any errors. Many writers read them orally to see if they "sound" right.

Directions: Read the following paragraph and look for any mechanical errors.

I enjoy living in a big old house in the country even though it is sandwiched in between a State Highway and the railroad tracks. Standing in front of this solidly built brick structure you can tell it is more than 100 years old and can imagine it will stand straight and square for another century. Once inside I don't really notice the heavy highway traffic the thick brick walls and overgrown forsythia bushes help to deaden the sound of tractor trailers and speeding cars. I especially like the inside of my house and its special features wide plank floors natural chestnut woodwork four working fireplaces and a huge eat-in kitchen. Everyone has their own bedroom in a large house and I can always find privacy in my roon. The railroad tracks are not visible as you walk out the back door. A row of poplar trees and evergreens sheild the view. Yes the trains are noisy when they pass, but after 16 years in this house, I don't even remember how often it goes by. Some people may prefer living in a city apartment or a quieter country road, but I could live in my house forever.

Check any areas below that might be problems in the paragraph. Be prepared to support your answers.

_____ Spelling _____ Capitalization _____ Other

_____ Grammar/Usage _____ Punctuation

Assignment: Revise and rewrite the paragraph. Eliminate any errors in mechanics.

_____
_____
_____
_____
_____
_____
_____

DW 26

Name_____

Date_____

REVISING II: EDITING

Information: Most writers are well aware of the need to make revisions of their first draft in the areas of spelling, punctuation, grammar, and usage. However, it is also important to check for other problems. Do you have an eye-catching introduction that previews the rest of the paragraph? Is your paragraph organized? You should not have repeated yourself or included information that is unrelated to the topic. Be sure to reread your first draft and look for any editorial errors.

Directions: Read the paragraph below and answer the questions that follow.

> Thanksgiving Day is one of my favorite holidays because the whole family gets together for a day of playing, talking, and feasting. Waiting until the traditional 3 p.m. serving time is agonizing. Just before sitting down to eat, I marvel at my mother's colorful display of food. It looks like a photograph from *Cuisine* Magazine: green leafy vegetables and salads, yellow squash and corn, golden brown turkey and duckling ready for my father's carving knife, crimson red beets and cranberry sauce, fluffy potatoes and stuffing, and deep, rich gravy. From the moment I wake I hear the clanging of pots and pans as well as the familiar hum of the dishwasher. It makes no difference what the weather is like outside because we stay inside most of the day. The smells of butterbasted turkey, fresh-baked rolls, and creamy pumpkin pies fill our house all day long. Even though breakfast and lunch are not served, we can snack on fresh fruits and vegetables, cheese, crackers, and nuts while patiently waiting for the main course. Despite our hunger, there is always more than enough food to feed this family of ten. Completely stuffed, my twin brother and I retire to our room to watch football games on television. I have the feeling I may never eat again, at least until early evening.

1. Is the introduction a general statement about the rest of the paragraph? _____ Why or why not? _____

_____

2. Are the details organized in a logical way? _____ If not, how could they be arranged? _____

_____

3. Do all the details relate to the introduction? _____ If not, which ones would you eliminate? _____

_____

4. Has any of the information been repeated? _____ If so, what could be eliminated? _____

_____

Assignment: Revise and rewrite the paragraph to eliminate any problems that exist.

_____

_____

_____

_____

_____

Name _____

Date _____

REVISING III: WORD CHOICE

Information: When you write the final draft of your descriptive paragraph, your main concern is in getting the ideas and organization on paper. Therefore, you do not always think of the best word or phrase to use at that time. Sometimes you put a word or phrase in the wrong place. Other times you may overuse a word or phrase. While reading over your first draft, substitute active verbs for inactive ones, replace overused or vague nouns with more precise ones, and try to eliminate unnecessary words or phrases.

Directions: Read the descriptive paragraph below. Circle any words that are overused. Cross out unnecessary words. Underline those words that could be expressed more accurately.

The most memorable part of the ferry ride to the Massachusetts island of Martha's Vineyard was watching the seagulls follow the boat. I was thoroughly entertained by watching several passengers tempt the birds with pieces of bread. They held their arms over the side of the boat and waited for the birds to take the bread out of their hands. Eight or ten birds hovered above the deck, waiting for the right moment to fly down and take the bread from the passengers' hands. I was impressed with how the birds rode the air currents, coasting effortlessly up and down and around. I was surprised at how quickly this 45-minute trip passed and I was determined to bring some bread of my own for the return trip.

Assignment: Revise and rewrite the paragraph by using more accurate and precise words.

DW 28

Name _____

Date _____

PRACTICE AND REVIEW I

Directions: Choose one of the topics below or use one of your own. In the spaces provided list any details that appeal to the senses. Next, write two different introductions, or leads, for your topic. Choose the better introduction and decide how to organize the notes.

1. A person in your class.
2. A trip into outer space.
3. Your first visit to the dentist.

Sight details _____

_____

Hearing details _____

_____

Touch details _____

_____

Taste details _____

_____

Smell details _____

_____

Introduction #1 _____

_____

_____

Introduction #2 _____

_____

_____

Type of organization _____

_____

Assignment: Write your first draft by organizing the notes above. Then write a descriptive paragraph (or paragraphs) about your topic. Remember to revise the first draft before writing the paragraph.

DW 29

Name _____

Date _____

PRACTICE AND REVIEW II

Directions: Choose one of the topics below or use one of your own. In the spaces provided, list any details that appeal to the senses. Next, write two different introductions, or leads, for your topic. Choose the better introduction and decide how to organize the notes.

1. A haunted house.
2. A sidewalk sale.
3. A brother, sister, or other family member.

Sight details _____

_____

Hearing details _____

_____

Touch details _____

_____

Taste details _____

_____

Smell details _____

_____

Introduction #1 _____

_____

_____

Introduction #2 _____

_____

_____

Type of organization _____

_____

Assignment: Write your first draft by organizing the notes above. Then write a descriptive paragraph (or paragraphs) about your topic. Remember to revise the first draft before writing the paragraph.

Name _____

Date _____

PRACTICE AND REVIEW III

Directions: Choose one of the topics below or use one of your own. In the spaces provided list any details that appeal to the senses. Next, write two different introductions, or leads, for your topic. Choose the better introduction and decide how to organize the notes.

1. A state, county, or town fair.
2. A rock concert.
3. Your favorite pastime or hobby.

Sight details _____

_____

Hearing details _____

_____

Touch details _____

_____

Taste details _____

_____

Smell details _____

_____

Introduction #1 _____

_____

_____

Introduction #2 _____

_____

_____

Type of organization _____

_____

Assignment: Write your first draft by organizing the notes above. Then write a descriptive paragraph (or paragraphs) about your topic. Remember to revise the first draft before writing the paragraph.

DW 31

Name _____

Date _____

PRACTICE AND REVIEW IV

Directions: Choose one of the topics below or use one of your own. In the spaces provided, list any details that appeal to the senses. Next, write two different introductions, or leads, for your topic. Choose the better introduction and decide how to organize the notes.

1. A fall (winter, spring, summer) day.
2. An amusement park.
3. Your best friend.

Sight details _____

_____

Hearing details _____

_____

Touch details _____

_____

Taste details _____

_____

Smell details _____

_____

Introduction #1 _____

_____

_____

Introduction #2 _____

_____

_____

Type of organization _____

_____

Assignment: Write your first draft by organizing the notes above. Then write a descriptive paragraph (or paragraphs) about your topic. Remember to revise the first draft before writing the paragraph.

DW 32

Name _____

Date _____

PRACTICE AND REVIEW V

Directions: Choose one of the topics below or use one of your own. In the spaces provided, list any details that appeal to the senses. Next, write two different introductions, or leads, for your topic. Choose the better introduction and decide how to organize the notes.

1. A restaurant you like.
2. An athletic contest or event.
3. What you would do if you won the lottery.

Sight details _____

Hearing details _____

Touch details _____

Taste details _____

Smell details _____

Introduction #1 _____

Introduction #2 _____

Type of organization _____

Assignment: Write your first draft by organizing the notes above. Then write a descriptive paragraph (or paragraphs) about your topic. Remember to revise the first draft before writing the paragraph.

DW 33

DESCRIPTIVE WRITING: OUTLINE FORM

Topic _____

Sight details _____

_____

_____

Hearing details _____

_____

_____

Touch details _____

_____

_____

Taste details _____

_____

_____

Smell details _____

_____

_____

Introduction (lead) #1 _____

_____

_____

Introduction (lead) #2 _____

_____

_____

Conclusion _____

_____

_____

Type of organization _____
     (position, time order, cause/effect)

DESCRIPTIVE WRITING TOPICS

1. Write about any spontaneous incidents.

2. Write about any pictures, photos, or objects.

3. Write about the person next to (beside, in front of) you.

4. Write a fable, such as "The Frog and the Waterfly."

5. Blindfold yourself and describe how something feels, tastes, smells, and sounds.

6. Without using any proper nouns, describe how to get from _____ (school, the post office) to _____ (home, the park).

7. "My trip to _____ was just incredible."

8. "As I woke up and came to my senses, I realized that I could not see."

9. "When I stepped around the corner onto Main Street, I could not believe what I was seeing."

10. "My life as a(n) _____ proved to be extremely dangerous."

11. "Our last camping trip was the most _____ weekend of my life."

12. "My life as a _____ (mouse, snake) was _____ ."

DESCRIPTIVE WRITING: SIGNAL WORDS

Connective
after	since
and	so
because	unless
before	until
but	when
for	while
if	yet
or	

Prepositions
aboard	behind	from	to
about	below	in	toward
above	beneath	into	under
across	beside	next to	underneath
against	between	of	up
along	beyond	off	upon
among	by	on	with
around	down	over	within
at	for	through	without

Time Order
after ...	earlier	next
afterwards	finally	second
at least	first	soon
at the same time	immediately	then
before ...	later	thereafter
before long	meanwhile	

Cause and Effect
as a result of	if—then
because	since
because of	so
caused by	therefore
consequently	thus
due to	when
for this reason	whenever

Position
above	crest	next to
across	down	peak
against	exterior	summit
at a distance	far	to (on) the left
base	foot	to (on) the right
behind	halfway	top
below	in back of	under
beneath	in front of	underneath
beside	interior	up
bottom	leading to	upward
close	near	

REPORT WRITING SKILLS AND ACTIVITIES

Categorizing I	RW 1
Categorizing II	RW 2
Topic Sentences and Details I	RW 3
Topic Sentences and Details II	RW 4
Details Unrelated to Topic	RW 5
Notes to Outline I	RW 6
Notes to Outline II	RW 7
Locating Subtopics and Details I	RW 8
Locating Subtopics and Details II	RW 9
Locating Subtopics and Details III	RW 10
Audience I	RW 11
Audience II	RW 12
Writing Introductions I	RW 13
Writing Introductions II	RW 14
Writing Conclusions I	RW 15
Writing Conclusions II	RW 16
From Notes to Sentences I	RW 17
From Notes to Sentences II	RW 18
Organizing by Sequence I	RW 19
Organizing by Sequence II	RW 20
Organizing by Sequence III	RW 21
Organizing by Comparing and Contrasting I	RW 22
Organizing by Comparing and Contrasting II	RW 23
Organizing by Comparing and Contrasting III	RW 24
Organizing by Comparing and Contrasting IV	RW 25
Organizing by Cause and Effect I	RW 26
Organizing by Cause and Effect II	RW 27
Organizing by Cause and Effect III	RW 28
Organizing by Cause and Effect IV	RW 29
Revising I: Mechanics	RW 30
Revising II: Editing	RW 31
Revising III: Word Choice	RW 32
Report Writing: Biography I	RW 33
Report Writing: Biography II	RW 34
Report Writing: Biography III	RW 35
Report Writing: Practice and Review I	RW 36
Report Writing: Practice and Review II	RW 37
Report Writing: Practice and Review III	RW 38
Report Writing: Practice and Review IV	RW 39
Report Writing: Practice and Review V	RW 40
Report Writing: Outline Form	RW 41
Report Writing: Topics	RW 42
Report Writing: Signal Words	RW 43

Name _____

Date _____

CATEGORIZING I

Directions: There are 22 words listed below. These words can be grouped together into four categories with one word in each group as the "topic word." Write the topic word on the line at the top of each group. The other words in the group are "subtopic words" and are examples of the topic. Write those words underneath the appropriate topic word.

Note: Some words might be used properly in more than one category. Be prepared to support your answers.

snake	butterfly	insect	wasp	giraffe
crab	animal	mosquito	fish	spider
goose	antelope	shrimp	bird	chicken
crow	cardinal	sparrow	trout	clam
	monkey		perch	

Topic Word: _____

_____
_____
_____
_____
_____
_____

Topic Word: _____

_____
_____
_____
_____
_____
_____

Topic Word: _____

_____
_____
_____
_____
_____
_____

Topic Word: _____

_____
_____
_____
_____
_____
_____

1. If you were to write a short one-paragraph report on each of these topics, how many paragraphs would you have? _____

2. What would be the topics of these paragraphs? _____

3. Write a topic sentence for one of the paragraphs. _____

4. Choose one of the categories and write a paragraph about it.

RW 1

Name _____

Date _____

CATEGORIZING II

Directions: There are 18 words or phrases listed below. These words or phrases can be listed or grouped together in three categories. One word or phrase in each group will be the "topic word." Write the topic word on the line next to the roman numeral. The other words listed are "subtopic words" and are examples of the topic. Write these words underneath the appropriate topic. Use a dictionary if necessary.

handsome	happiness	feelings	applaud
comfortable	clumsy	muscular	tall
excitement	athletic	behavior	sorrow
compliment	ignore	joy	obese
physical characteristics	argue		

I. _____

II. _____

III. _____

1. If you were to write a short one-paragraph report on each of these groups of words, how many paragraphs would you have? _____
2. What would be the topics of these paragraphs? _____

3. Write a topic sentence for each of the paragraphs.
   I. _____
   II. _____
   III. _____

4. Now write *one* paragraph using one of your topic sentences and its subtopic words.

RW 2

Name _____

Date _____

TOPIC SENTENCES AND DETAILS I

Directions: Below you will read some details about an event. However, the notes do *not* include a main topic. *After reading* the notes, identify the topic of the information. *Then* write a good topic sentence. *Finally,* use this topic sentence as the beginning of a paragraph. Be sure to include all the notes in the paragraph and feel free to add your own ideas. Be sure to write in complete sentences.

Notes

chickens scurried to their pen
leaves rustled around the yard
my mother hurried to put garden tools away
huge, low-flying black clouds in western sky
bolt of lightning cracked in distance
gusts of wind blew open barn door
Father ran inside to close windows

Topic: _____

Topic Sentence: _____

RW 3

Name _____

Date _____

TOPIC SENTENCES AND DETAILS II

Directions: Read the four topic sentences listed below:

1. The last trip we took to _____ was _____.
2. My weekday schedule is monotonous and boring.
3. There are several reasons why _____ is my favorite season of the year.
4. On my way to school there are so many _____ sights to see.

Directions: Choose two of the topic sentences and expand each topic with seven specific details. List the details in the chart below.

Topic I: _____   Topic II: _____

D	D
E	E
T	T
A	A
I	I
L	L
S	S

Assignment: Write a four-to-six sentence paragraph using one of the topics above. Be sure to start with the topic sentence. Also make sure that your details follow in complete sentences.

_____
_____
_____
_____
_____
_____
_____
_____
_____

RW 4

Name _____

Date _____

DETAILS UNRELATED TO TOPIC

Directions: Read the following paragraphs carefully. Look for any problems in the paragraphs.

    There are several advantages to owning a small car these days, yet there are still many good reasons why some people prefer to drive a larger car.

    The benefits of a small car in today's world should be obvious. Most important, the ever-increasing cost of fuel encourages us to use less gas. Let's not be controlled by foreign oil producers. Smaller, lighter cars are much more fuel efficient than large cars, and some will even give you 50 miles on a gallon of gasoline. Since the car is smaller, it should cost us less to buy, operate, and maintain. If we want to reduce our dependence on foreign oil, then cutting gasoline usage is an effective way to do this.

    However, an argument can be made in favor of big cars, too. A family larger than three or four would feel cramped in a small car, especially on a long trip. In addition, some people are convinced that large cars are safer and offer more protection than small ones. My whole family owns small cars. Furthermore, they say, you can enjoy a more comfortable ride in a heavier, larger vehicle. Those people who travel extensively like a comfortable car. The government cannot make us buy small cars.

    In conclusion, each car buyer must make a decision as to which kind of car to buy after considering all of the advantages of each and his or her own needs. Which one would you choose?

What problems do you see in these paragraphs? Check the spaces below if you think there is a problem.

_____ 1. No introduction   _____ 3. Topic not clear

_____ 2. No conclusion   _____ 4. Details unrelated to topic

If you checked number four you are correct. There are sentences in paragraphs two and three that are NOT related to the topic sentences. <u>Underline</u> those sentences you feel are not related in each paragraph.

Are there any other problems in these paragraphs? Be specific. Share your responses.

_____
_____
_____
_____
_____
_____
_____
_____
_____

RW 5

Name _____

Date _____

NOTES TO OUTLINE I

Directions: Listed below are several notes about birds. Three of these notes are listed as subtopics in the "Outline on Birds" which follows the notes. Write the details from the notes for each subtopic on the lines under A, B, and C.

Notes on Birds

> Some birds travel thousands of miles to exact locations.
>
> The physical characteristics of birds are very noticeable.
>
> Their singing ability sets them apart from other animals.
>
> Others have a low, raucous sound.
>
> Mankind has been amazed at their ability to fly.
>
> A number of birds imitate others when they sing.
>
> These habits vary among birds, but they all follow regular routes.
>
> Certain migratory habits are peculiar to birds.
>
> Some birds' songs are high and shrill sounding.
>
> Their feathery covering comes in many sizes and colors.

Outline on Birds

A. The physical characteristics of birds are very noticeable.

  1. _____

  2. _____

B. Their singing ability sets them apart from other animals.

  1. _____

  2. _____

  3. _____

C. Certain migratory habits are peculiar to birds.

  1. _____

  2. _____

Assignment: Write these notes in sentences and paragraphs. How many paragraphs will you have? Add relevant information if you want to expand the paragraph(s).

RW 6

Name _____

Date _____

NOTES TO OUTLINE II

Directions: Listed below are notes about colonial fireplaces. Three of the notes are subtopics which you should write on lines A, B, and C in the outline following the notes. The other notes are details about each of the subtopics. Write these on the numbered lines below A, B, and C.

Notes for "How Colonial Fireplaces Were Used"

> Hardwoods such as oak and maple gave the best heat.
>
> Loaves of bread were baked in metal ovens built into the fireplace.
>
> Children played games nearby.
>
> Heating the house was an important use of the fireplace.
>
> The fireplace was the center of family life during the winter.
>
> Meat was roasted on a spit.
>
> A huge supply of wood was burned during cold weather.
>
> The family read the Bible and other books before the fire.
>
> The fireplace was used for all the cooking of the food.
>
> Vegetables were stewed in boiling pots hanging over the fire.
>
> Ears of corn and potatoes were roasted in the hot ashes.
>
> Visitors were entertained before the fire.

Outline for "How Colonial Fireplaces Were Used"

A. _____
   1. _____
   2. _____
   3. _____
   4. _____

B. _____
   1. _____
   2. _____
   3. _____

C. _____
   1. _____
   2. _____

Assignment: Write these notes in sentences and paragraphs. How many paragraphs will you have? Add relevant information if you want to expand the paragraph(s).

RW 7

Name _____

Date _____

LOCATING SUBTOPICS AND DETAILS I

Directions: Read the following topic sentence:

"We can observe a number of different geometrical shapes in our daily lives."

Now read the notes listed below. There are three subtopics among the notes. Also, there are several details or examples of each subtopic. On the lines to the left of the notes, label the subtopics A, B, and C. Finally, write A-1, A-2, A-3, B-1, etc. next to the details that tell about each topic.

Notes

_____ steering wheels and tires

_____ spend many hours a week in front of television

_____ many examples of rectangular shapes to observe

_____ sails on sailboats, many tents are this shape

_____ even houses themselves have this shape

_____ circular shapes seen everywhere

_____ some men wear neckties with this kind of shape

_____ doors, windows examples of four-sided shape

_____ doughnuts eaten at breakfast

_____ shapes that resemble triangles are hard to find

_____ play games with balls of different sizes

_____ if live in city see many radio and TV towers

Assignment: Using the topic sentence above, write a paragraph or paragraphs including the subtopics and details you have numbered and lettered.

RW 8

Name _____

Date _____

LOCATING SUBTOPICS AND DETAILS II

Directions: Read the following topic sentence:

"Mark Twain was one of America's most creative and prolific writers."

Now read the notes listed below. There are three subtopics among the notes. Also, there are several details or examples of each subtopic. On the lines to the left of the notes, label the subtopics A, B, and C. Finally, write A-1, A-2, A-3, B-1, etc. next to the details that tell about each subtopic.

Notes

_____ during Civil War, worked on newspaper Virginia City, Nevada

_____ early life had great influence on later years

_____ father died 1847 leaving family in need of support

_____ started work career as journalist and newspaperman

_____ storytelling ability important throughout career

_____ became quite wealthy from sale of books

_____ finished only six years of school; began work at age 12

_____ first worked for *Hannibal Journal* as apprentice printer for brother

_____ raised near Mississippi River, which was setting for many writings

_____ two best novels: *Tom Sawyer* and *Huck Finn*

_____ after Civil War traveled in Europe and wrote news stories about trip

_____ from 1869-1896 published series of books and stories

Assignment: Using the topic sentence above, write a paragraph or paragraphs including the subtopics and details you have numbered and lettered.

RW 9

Name _____

Date _____

LOCATING SUBTOPICS AND DETAILS III

Directions: Read the notes that are randomly listed in the box below. They include three subtopics along with several details or examples that relate to each subtopic. The main topic is *not* given. On the lines to the left of the notes, label the three subtopics A, B, and C. Then write A-1, A-2, A-3, B-1, etc. next to the details that tell about each subtopic.

Notes

_____	Doesn't require viewers to think
_____	Children may be misled by tricky or false advertising
_____	Television can be very entertaining and relaxing
_____	News reports keep us in touch with what's happening all around the world
_____	We can also learn much from television
_____	Programs like "National Geographic" are very informative as well as enjoyable
_____	Fun to watch people compete on game shows
_____	Programs that glorify violence and crime can influence a person's behavior
_____	Both kids and adults enjoy sports programs of all kinds
_____	On the other hand, television can have many harmful effects
_____	Keeps students from schoolwork and reading for pleasure
_____	Many children learn about history and literature by watching programs like "Little House on the Prairie"

Write a topic sentence for these notes: _____

_____

Assignment: Using these notes, write a report for your social studies class. Organize the A's, B's, and C's into separate paragraphs. Don't forget to write an introduction and a conclusion.

RW 10

Name _____

Date _____

AUDIENCE I

Directions: Below are listed the facts about an accident that occurred recently in Springdale. You observed the accident as you were getting ready to cross an intersection.

Saturday, March 19, 1983, 6:30 p.m.
Sports car filled with young people driving behind station wagon
Elderly man and woman in station wagon driving south on Smith Street
Station wagon slowed down as if to stop
Sports car pulled out, accelerated to pass on left
No other cars on road
Station wagon turned left
Sports car tried to avoid wagon and crashed into tree
Station wagon made turn and came to stop

The information above is a series of facts. No judgments have been made about them. Read the two paragraphs about the incident and answer the questions that follow.

Paragraph A

As I was about to cross the intersection of Smith Street and Main Street in the Village of Springdale last Saturday, March 19, 1983, at 6:30 p.m., I observed the following. I first noticed a dark station wagon slowing down as it approached the intersection. It appeared that the car, driven by an elderly man, was going to stop. Then I saw a sports car pull outside to the left and accelerate, as if to pass. I could see there were several people in it. Next, the station wagon turned left and into the path of the faster-moving sports car. The driver of the sports car swerved away to avoid the other car and drove directly into a large tree. The wagon completed its turn and came to a stop without being hit.

Paragraph B

You wouldn't believe what I saw last Saturday night as I left Jennifer's house! This beat-up station wagon was creeping along Main Street to the corner of Smith Street. You really couldn't tell what the old goat who was driving was going to do. Next thing I heard and saw was Paul Jay's neat-looking Trans-Am pull around the wagon to pass. Well, that idiot in the wagon started to turn left and cut right in front of Paul's car. Paul swerved to avoid him and rammed right into that old maple tree on the corner. There were quite a few kids in Paul's car, but I guess no one was hurt seriously. You just can't trust these old people driving cars!

Questions:

1. Who was the audience in Paragraph A? _____

   Paragraph B? _____

2. Who was at fault according to Paragraph A? _____

   Paragraph B? _____

3. What kinds of judgments and opinions were made in Paragraph B that were not made in Paragraph A?

   _____

   _____

RW 11

Name _____

Date _____

AUDIENCE II

Directions: Below are listed the facts about an accident that occurred recently in Springdale. The facts are the same as those listed in "Audience I."

Saturday, March 19, 1983, 6:30 p.m.
Sports car filled with young people driving behind station wagon
Elderly man and woman in station wagon driving south on Smith St.
Station wagon slowed down as if to stop
Sports car pulled out, accelerated to pass on left
No other cars on road
Station wagon turned left
Sports car tried to avoid wagon and crashed into tree
Station wagon made turn and came to stop

The information above is a series of facts. No judgments or opinions have been made about the people or objects involved. No judgment has been made about who is at fault.

Pretend that you are a 60-year-old man who has just left his bridge club and observes the accident on his way home. Write a description of the accident to a close friend. Write this description in a way that blames the young people for the accident.

RW 12

Name _____

Date _____

WRITING INTRODUCTIONS I

Directions: Read the following situation for writing a report and compare it to the sample introduction. Then answer the questions that follow.

Situation: The principal, guidance counselor, and members of the English department are considering changing the present English curriculum. They have asked you to interview members of the student body to find out their opinion about changing from one 40-week subject to two 20-week subjects. You will then report your findings to the board of education.

Sample Introduction:

"As a member of the student council, I was asked by the principal, guidance counselor, and English department to interview students about a change in the English department curriculum. This change would allow students to choose two 20-week courses, rather than being assigned one 40-week course in English. The information below will highlight how the students feel about this proposed change."

How is the introduction similar to the situation? _____

How does the introduction differ from the situation? _____

Directions: Read the following situation for writing a report. Then write your own introduction.

Situation: You are the student council representative to the board of education. The board has discussed at its monthly meeting the possibility of *not* allowing students to drive their cars to school. You took notes on the discussion and now must report back to the student council the ideas discussed by the board.

Introduction:

_____
_____
_____
_____
_____
_____
_____
_____
_____
_____

RW 13

Name _____

Date _____

WRITING INTRODUCTIONS II

Directions: The notes listed in the box below relate to the second situation described in Writing Introductions I. These notes will give you more information to include in an introduction. Read and organize the notes, then complete the assignment that follows.

Notes

> Middle Valley High School cafeteria
>
> April 8, 1983
>
> students have constitutional right to drive
>
> most student driving is unnecessary
>
> might have to buy additional buses to carry extra students
>
> quite a bit of disagreement on this topic
>
> some students need quick transportation to after-school jobs
>
> participants in extracurricular activities have unusual hours
>
> superintendent asked a committee to look into pros and cons of this action
>
> some use cars as escape to drink and/or take drugs
>
> "All this extra driving is a waste of energy," according to Phil Hulton, taxpayer and parent

Assignment: Rewrite your introduction, if necessary, and then write the notes above as a report to the student council. Remember that as a reporter you are not supposed to include any of your own opinions in a report. You should include only facts from the meeting.

RW 14

Name _____

Date _____

WRITING CONCLUSIONS I

Directions: Read the situation, sample introduction, and sample conclusion in Part A below. Notice how they are similar and how they are different. Discuss Part A with a partner, your teacher, or the class. Then read the situation and introduction for Part B and write a conclusion.

PART A:

Situation: You are a reporter for the school newspaper, the *Eagle Eye*, and you attended the November 17th AFS meeting. The foreign exchange student, Heidi Gensler, compared and contrasted life in Germany and in the United States. You wrote a news article for the *Eagle Eye* about this event.

Introduction: As your traveling reporter for the *Eagle Eye*, I attended the recent AFS meeting to hear our German exchange student, Miss Heidi Gensler. She presented a very humorous and informative lecture comparing American and German lifestyles.

Conclusion: In short, last Thursday's AFS meeting was one of the best in memory. Heidi's ability to make us laugh and listen at the same time made the hour-long presentation seem like five minutes. For those of you who could not attend, I hope you take the time to get to know Heidi.

PART B:

Situation: Your Modern Cultures class has been studying many different cultures throughout the world. The teacher has asked you to attend "Italian Night" and report your experiences to the rest of the class. All profits from this event, sponsored by the Hillside Rotary Club, will be donated to the Muscular Dystrophy Foundation. Many Rotarians will bring an Italian dish to share with others. Mr. Angelo Sabatini will also conduct a slide presentation on Italy.

Introduction: The Hillside Rotary Club sponsored "Italian Night" at the Hillside Regional High School last Wednesday night for the benefit of the Muscular Dystrophy Foundation. After the excellent dinner, Mr. Angelo Sabatini conducted a very educational slide presentation on the "People and Culture of Italy."

Conclusion:

_____

_____

_____

_____

RW 15

Name _____

Date _____

WRITING CONCLUSIONS II

Information: Writing a conclusion is like writing someone a reminder. That is, you are reminding that person of what you have said before in just a few short words. Choosing those few short words is the key to writing a good conclusion. To find the words, do this: (1) identify the subtopics of your notes, (2) circle the key words in those subtopics, and (3) use those key words in your conclusion.

Directions: Read the notes on radar listed below. Identify subtopics A, B, and C. Circle the key words and use them in your conclusion. You may also want to use the "Conclusion Signal Words" shown in the box below to help you get started with the conclusion.

Notes on Radar

- ____ helps control airplane traffic at major airports
- ____ first developed 1935-40 as system for detecting position of remote objects by radio waves
- ____ used to navigate warships and bombers in all kinds of weather
- ____ peacetime uses of radar similar to military uses
- ____ improved immensely after World War II
- ____ can detect enemy aircraft at several hundred miles
- ____ military uses play important role in country's defense
- ____ used as aid in navigating large cargo ships in harbors
- ____ uses as a navigation and detection tool continuing to expand
- ____ also used for short-term weather forecasting
- ____ used in early warning system to protect North America from air invasion
- ____ newest use is in study of planets

Conclusion Signal Words

in conclusion	finally	consequently
in summary	in short	therefore
as you can see	to sum up	the information given above

Now write your conclusion:

_____

_____

_____

_____

RW 16

Name _____

Date _____

FROM NOTES TO SENTENCES I

Information: Usually notes for a report are *not* taken in sentence and paragraph form. We jot them down quickly and in no specific order. When we want to use the notes we must first organize them by subtopic and detail. Then we need to rewrite them in complete sentences. When we do the rewriting, we ask ourselves three questions:

1. Are there any missing words, capital letters, or punctuation?
2. Can I combine any of the notes into one sentence?
3. Can I add any supplementary information or words?

Directions: Read and organize the following notes on your class trip to the Museum of Natural History. Asking yourself the three questions above, rewrite the notes in complete sentences.

Notes on Class Trip

> Thursday morning, October 14, 1982
> stopped at fast-food restaurant for lunch
> wondered how people could have lived with so little machinery
> took school bus to museum of Natural History in Rochester
> wandered about museum for nearly two hours
> different artifacts and remnants of early civilizations
> Mr. Wetzel's social studies class went on field trip
> amazed at old tools—could we use today?
> class has studied several ancient civilizations
> discussed trip when we returned to class
> saw model of Egyptian shadoof, used to irrigate fields

RW 17

Name _____

Date _____

FROM NOTES TO SENTENCES II

Information: Usually notes taken for a report are *not* written in sentence form. We jot them down quickly and in no specific order. First, you should organize the notes according to a plan. Then you should rewrite them in complete sentences.

Directions: Read the notes listed below. Number the notes in the order in which *you* think they happened. Then rewrite the notes in complete sentences. Remember to ask yourself three questions:

1. Are there any missing words, capital letters, or punctuation?
2. Can I combine any of the notes into one sentence?
3. Can I add any supplementary information or words?

Notes on Elizabeth Blackwell

- ___ Elizabeth Blackwell, born 1819, died 1910
- ___ real pioneer in struggle for women's rights
- ___ started medical college to train women
- ___ first woman doctor in U.S.
- ___ very determined—would not give up
- ___ accepted Geneva College of Medicine, Geneva, NY
- ___ study continued—Paris, France; London, England
- ___ very successful—worked hard for what she wanted
- ___ practiced medicine in New York City first
- ___ received first medical degree 1849—high honors
- ___ wanted to study medicine—no school would let her
- ___ established hospital—treated women and children

_____
_____
_____
_____
_____
_____
_____
_____
_____
_____

RW 18

Name _____

Date _____

ORGANIZING BY SEQUENCE I

Information: Writers present their material in several different ways. If their information is presented in a time order, we say that it follows a sequence. Many kinds of written material follow this pattern including news articles, police reports, and history books.

Directions: First, read the paragraph below and look for any words or phrases that signal time order or sequence. Then circle those words.

Mrs. James Wilson was guided to safety yesterday when a flight instructor radioed instructions for her to land the Piper Cub airplane in which she was a passenger. Mr. Wilson had collapsed from a heart attack while flying the single-engine plane home from their mountain vacation home. Immediately thereafter, Mrs. Wilson panicked. Then she yelled over the radio for someone to help her. At that time, a flight instructor just happened to hear her screams. First, he tried to calm her down by explaining the controls. Next, he helped her locate the position of the plane. He finally guided her in the right direction and convinced her that she could land the plane without any major problems. After a bumpy landing and a terrifying experience, Mrs. Wilson told reporters, "I guess somebody was with us up there!"

Directions: There are several words listed in the box below that act as time signals. Write your own account of an event that has taken place in or about your school or home. Use some of these time signals in your account. If you cannot think of a topic, look at your local newspaper for ideas.

first	then	after	immediately
next	when	before	simultaneously
finally	while	until	subsequently
last	as soon as	thereafter	at that time
	during		

_____
_____
_____
_____
_____
_____
_____
_____
_____
_____

RW 19

Name _____

Date _____

ORGANIZING BY SEQUENCE II

Directions: Read the situation and notes below, then write a report based on them. Present that report in the sequence or time-order organizational pattern. Use the sequence signal words. They help!

Situation: You attended the rock concert at the Carver High Auditorium. As a reporter for the school newspaper, you have to write an article about the concert for next week's edition.

Notes

- ____ 12 people injured at rock concert
- ____ played many hit tunes flawlessly for 2½ hours
- ____ "Seats for future concerts will all be reserved," according to promoter John Horgan
- ____ "Wayward Wrecking Company" performed December 3 at Carver High Auditorium
- ____ crowd pushed and shoved to get tickets and best seats
- ____ concert went on, as scheduled, but late start
- ____ injured people rushed to River Road Hospital
- ____ band not aware of what happened until after concert
- ____ only a few seats reserved out of 1500 in auditorium

Assignment: Organize these notes according to sequence. Combine any notes that could go together in one sentence. Use any sequence signal words you need to make the article clear and accurate.

_____

_____

_____

_____

_____

_____

_____

_____

_____

_____

_____

_____

RW 20

Name _____

Date _____

ORGANIZING BY SEQUENCE III

Directions: Read the situation and notes below, then write a report based on them. Present that report in the sequence, or time-order pattern of organization. Use the sequence signal words ... they help!

Situation: You are one of four students in a geography class who took cross-country trips with their families last summer, beginning in New York State. Each of you will write a report to present to the class, so the entire class can compare your experiences.

Notes

____	visited Astrodome in Houston—watched Astros beat Mets
____	while in California, went to Disneyland and Hollywood
____	drove west to Grand Canyon National Park, Arizona—camped for two days
____	younger brother broke his leg at campsite near Cincinnati—got special treatment the rest of way home
____	our trip across country last summer was long but memorable
____	went southwest through Tennessee, Arkansas to Texas
____	family decided to visit Mount St. Helens in Washington even though we hadn't planned to go farther north
____	on to Las Vegas—won $50 in slot machine near campsite
____	drove across Midwest—couldn't believe the land in Iowa, Illinois, Indiana so flat—went miles without seeing a hill
____	began trip back east through Idaho to Yellowstone Park—camped two days at Old Faithful
____	drove up Pacific Coast to San Francisco—took great pictures of Bay Area Bridge
____	took trail down Grand Canyon to Colorado River—explored Indian pueblos
____	drove south through beautiful Blue Ridge Mountains of Virginia—camped there three days
____	trip from Las Vegas to Los Angeles through Mojave Desert helped me appreciate water and plant life

Assignment: Write this report according to the sequence of events. Use any sequence signal words you need to make your report clear and accurate.

RW 21

Name _____

Date _____

ORGANIZING BY COMPARING AND CONTRASTING I

Information: Writers present their material in several different ways. If their writing shows how things or ideas are alike or different, they compare or contrast these things or ideas. Many types of written material, including social studies and science books, follow this pattern.

Directions: First read the paragraph below and look for any words or phrases that seem to compare or contrast the important ideas. Circle those words or phrases. Finally, answer the questions that follow.

The high schools of America are alike in many ways, yet there are some obvious differences among them. Most high schools are similar in that they require students to take basic subjects such as English, mathematics, social studies, and physical education. On the other hand, elective, or nonrequired, subjects vary greatly from school to school. City high schools often include only grades 10-12. In contrast, high schools in many rural towns or villages cover grades 7-12. Although there are a number of other differences among the schools, they all share the same basic goal—to prepare their students for the future.

1. What is being compared and contrasted? _____

2. In the paragraph above, what words or phrases signal when an idea will be compared or contrasted? List them below:

_____

_____

Directions: Choosing one of the topics below, or any other topic you may prefer, write a paragraph *comparing* and/or *contrasting* two things or ideas. You may use any of the signal words found in the box at the bottom of the page.

1. softball and baseball
2. two members of your family
3. eating at home and at a restaurant
4. _____?_____

Signal Words That Help Compare and Contrast		
similarly	in the same way	likewise
compared to	on the other hand	in contrast
in like manner	contrasted with	on the contrary

RW 22

Name _____

Date _____

ORGANIZING BY COMPARING AND CONSTRASTING II

Directions: Read the situation and notes below, then, using the compare/contrast organizational pattern, write a report based on this information. Use the compare/contrast signal words ... they help!

Situation: You have recorded the notes below from many resources you found in the library and elsewhere. Use them to write a *one-paragraph* report on coal and oil for your geology teacher.

Notes

- large supply of coal in U.S. greater than oil
- oil needs to be pumped out of ground
- two fossil fuels—coal and oil—have greater reserves than all other countries
- oil must be processed before used
- coal used basically for generating energy
- large percentage of oil comes from foreign countries
- coal dug out of deep mines or stripped from surface
- coal doesn't need any special treatment before use
- oil used in production of many products, such as plastics and lubricants

Assignment: Organize these notes by subtopic so you can compare and contrast the important ideas. Which notes go together? Then write a good topic sentence. Finally, use the compare/contrast signal words to help you organize the information in your one paragraph.

_____
_____
_____
_____
_____
_____
_____
_____
_____
_____

RW 23

Name _____

Date _____

ORGANIZING BY COMPARING AND CONTRASTING III

Directions: Read the situation and notes below. Then, using the compare/contrast organizational pattern, **write a** report based on the information given. Use the compare/contrast signal words ... they help!

Situation: You have recorded the notes below during class and from information booklets on each of three sports. Your gym teacher wants you to write a report which will be presented to several foreign exchange students who will be attending your school.

Notes

> 11 players each side wearing heavy, protective equipment
>
> played on diamond-shaped field which varies in size
>
> football played in fall with professional championship games extending into January
>
> basketball is fast-moving sport usually played in gym during winter months
>
> played on field 100 yards long (excluding end zones) and 53 yards wide
>
> three very popular sports enjoyed by Americans throughout the year
>
> professional baseball season begins April—lasts until October with World Series
>
> object to score touchdown worth six points, plus one point for the extra kick, and field goals worth three points
>
> five players per team play both offense and defense
>
> object to get as many batters as possible to hit ball safely and score runs
>
> nine players space themselves around field to prevent opponents from hitting ball safely and scoring runs
>
> all of these games played in schools, on playgrounds, and by professionals
>
> object to score the most baskets in four quarters of play

Assignment: Organize these notes by subtopic so you can compare and contrast the important ideas. Use the compare/contrast signal words in your paragraphs.

RW 24

Name _____

Date _____

ORGANIZING BY COMPARING AND CONTRASTING IV

Directions: Read the situation and notes below. Then, using the compare/contrast organizational pattern, write a report based on the information given. Use the compare/contrast signal words ... they help!

Situation: You have been asked by your health teacher to prepare a report on different kinds of drugs. This report will be presented to the fifth and sixth graders to inform them about the dangers of drug abuse.

Notes

> stimulants are drugs that speed action of central nervous system
>
> under drug influence we lose self-control—don't know what we're doing
>
> barbiturates, known as "downers," slow reflexes, make sleepy
>
> LSD, hashish, and PCP or "Angel Dust," can cause us to hallucinate, see things not there
>
> long-term use of cocaine may cause depression, convulsions
>
> all these drugs lead to mental dependency—hard to break
>
> even mild depressants like alcohol, tobacco harmful to bodies
>
> two examples of stimulants: cocaine and amphetamines
>
> heroin and morphine are opiates—highly addictive, physically and mentally dangerous
>
> hallucinogens change person's idea of what's happening
>
> depressants such as barbiturates and opiates slow down central nervous system
>
> "speed" is stimulant causing increased heart rate and pulse

Assignment: Organize these notes by subtopic so you can compare and contrast the important ideas. Use the compare/contrast signal words in your paragraphs.

RW 25

Name _____

Date _____

ORGANIZING BY CAUSE AND EFFECT I

Information: Writers present their written material in several different ways. One of the patterns they use shows how certain events or ideas can *cause*, or lead to, another event. Many types of written material, including newspaper articles and science textbooks, follow this pattern.

Directions: First, read the paragraph below. Then look for any words or phrases that might signal when one event causes something else to happen. Circle those words or phrases. Finally, answer the questions that follow.

The early morning fire of April 10 at the Midlakes Junior High School has resulted in many problems for the district. Due to the intense heat generated from the fire, there was a great deal of structural damage to the auditorium. Consequently, most of the beams supporting the walls and the roof of this area must be replaced. Since smoke damage was very heavy in the seventh-grade wing of the building, all seventh-grade classes have had to be transferred to the Methodist Church Annex until further notice. Many citizens are upset because the newly installed fire alarm system failed to work properly, allowing the fire to burn out of control for nearly two hours before the fire department arrived. As a result of the fire, Superintendent of Schools, Dr. Philip Holgado, decided to close the school three days before the regularly scheduled spring vacation. This will allow the cleanup crew a few extra days to prepare for reopening on April 23.

1. List the words or phrases that you circled. _____

_____

2. How many of those words or phrases are included in the box of cause/effect signal words shown below?

_____

Directions: Choosing one of the topics listed below or any other topic you may prefer, write a cause/effect paragraph. You will find it helpful to use some of the signal words in the box at the bottom of this page.

1. a traffic accident
2. the blizzard of 1982
3. a power blackout
4. your choice

Cause and Effect Signal Words			
since	because of	thus	caused by
due to	consequently	so	as a result
because	therefore	if—then	for this reason

RW 26

Name _____

Date _____

ORGANIZING BY CAUSE AND EFFECT II

Directions: Read the situation and notes below and write a report that uses the cause/effect organizational pattern. Use the cause/effect signal words. They help!

Situation: As a reporter for the *Valley View Herald*, you interviewed the mayor of Lower Malta after a recent storm. Your notes from the interview are in the box below.

Notes

- overtime pay for city and county workers
- bridge to hospital swept into river
- local economy to suffer
- winter wheat crop destroyed
- Malta River overflowed
- several farmers in lower valley lost livestock and machinery
- will take many days to restore electric power
- drinking water may be unsafe—must boil
- early crops and fertilizers washed away
- used up all emergency fund money in budget
- Mayor Wilson requested all citizens to work together to recover from disaster

Assignment: First organize the notes by subtopic so you can group them in your paragraph(s). Then write a good topic sentence. Finally, use the cause/effect signal words in your paragraph(s) to help organize the information according to this pattern.

RW 27

Name _____

Date _____

ORGANIZING BY CAUSE AND EFFECT III

Directions: Read the situation and notes below to write a report that uses the cause/effect organizational pattern. Use the cause/effect signal words ... they help!

Situation: The students in a twelfth-grade health class have studied "Nutrition and Its Effect on Performance." They have also taken a survey of students and their eating habits. Some of the results of their study and survey are listed in the following notes. You have been asked to report these findings to the board of education.

Notes

students eat poorly the rest of the day

39% of students surveyed had no breakfast at all

students "high" on sugar can be behavior problems

overweight people suffer from poor circulation, bad feet, and backaches

even at home, snacks eaten were low in food value

many come to school without a well-balanced breakfast

78% of those who eat school lunches do not eat the vegetables, fruits, or salads

those without breakfast feel "lazy" and cannot concentrate

snacks included foods high in sugar, salt and carbonation

diabetes and high blood pressure can result from poor diet

our feeling that board of education and parents should look further into this problem

those who eat breakfast consume high quantities of sugar and carbohydrates

can lead to school and health problems

Assignment: Organize these notes by subtopics so you can group the important ideas, using the cause/effect pattern. Then write a good introduction. Finally, use the cause/effect signal words to help you organize the information in paragraphs.

RW 28

Name _____

Date _____

ORGANIZING BY CAUSE AND EFFECT IV

Directions: Read the situation and notes below and write a report using the <u>cause/effect</u> organizational pattern. Use the cause/effect signal words ... they help!

Situation: As a member of the Work Study Program at school, you are required to write a report to the class about your experiences as a student nurse at the Wayne County Memorial Hospital. You wrote the following notes in preparing this report.

Notes

- all volunteer—no pay
- nurses don't panic, even under emergency conditions
- must be good listener and encourage patients to talk about themselves
- worked as student nurse afternoons since September
- learned great deal about organization and operation of hospital
- like to become registered nurse
- met many friendly and dedicated people
- nurses really run each floor and ward like clockwork
- respect patience and knowledge of nursing staff
- must not get too personally involved with patients and problems
- hope to work in hospital full-time some day

Assignment: Organize these notes by subtopic so you can group the important ideas, using the cause/effect organizational pattern. Then write a good introduction. Finally, use the cause/effect signal words to help you organize the information in paragraphs.

RW 29

Name _____

Date _____

REVISING I: MECHANICS

Information: When you write the first draft of a report, you are usually most interested in organizing the information in sentences and paragraphs. It is only natural to make mechanical errors in spelling, punctuation, capitalization, and grammar. Thus, it is important to read through the first draft carefully, looking for such errors. Many people read the first draft orally to see if it "sounds" right.

Directions: Read the paragraph below and look for any mechanical errors.

In our society, we do not live independantly of each other. A farmer in iowa may use a combine made in detroit michigan that Assembly line workers in detroit may wear clothes made from cotton grown by Alabama farmers and manufactured by workers in New York. The workers in New York will likely eat bread made from the wheat harvested by the Iowa farmer. we all depend on other people from different parts of the county for the things they need and want.

Check the kinds of errors that have been made in the paragraph:

_____ spelling _____ capitalization _____ words omitted

_____ punctuation _____ grammar _____ other

Assignment: Make any corrections necessary in the paragraph. Read it out loud to yourself to help you find any errors. Finally, rewrite the paragraph in final draft form.

_____

_____

_____

_____

_____

_____

_____

_____

RW 30

Name _____

Date _____

REVISING II: EDITING

Information: When you write the first draft of a report, you are usually most interested in getting the information on paper. Sometimes you will put words or phrases in the wrong places, repeat ideas, forget to write an introduction or a conclusion, include unrelated information, or even write in a disorganized way. It is important to read your draft, looking for any of these problems.

Directions: Read the paragraph below and look for any editorial errors. Then check any problem areas that are included in the list following the paragraph.

Last Thursday I interviewed Dr. Jack Harris, after his entertaining and thoughtful assembly program on drug abuse in the Valleyview High School Auditorium. "This building does not look 15 years old. It's been well cared for," he remarked. Likewise, the whole school community appreciated his sense of humor and the message he left with us. His comments about our school were very complimentary. He was impressed with the condition and cleanliness of the school itself. Dr. Harris also made several positive statements about the students. "Their behavior and attention during the assembly was the best I have experienced in my eleven years of talking to students," he noted. Obviously, Dr. Harris enjoyed his short stay at Valleyview High School. The students' standing ovation at the conclusion of the assembly was especially satisfying to him.

_____ organization   _____ repetition of ideas
_____ words out of place   _____ introduction
_____ unrelated information   _____ conclusion

Assignment: Now rewrite the paragraph after editing any problems.

_____
_____
_____
_____
_____
_____
_____
_____
_____
_____

Name _____

Date _____

REVISING III: WORD CHOICE

Information: When you write the first draft of a report you are usually most interested in getting the information on paper. Therefore you don't always think of the best word or phrase to use.

Directions: Read the report below and underline any words or phrases that can be better expressed in fewer or more precise words. Also cross out any unnecessary words.

We had "Career Planning Day" at our school last week. It was sponsored by the Guidance Department, and many representatives from many areas spoke to us.

An Air Force recruiter said the Air Force was an excellent opportunity for advancement, for education, and for experience. However, the Navy recruiter said their program offered technical skill training and an opportunity to travel throughout the world. Several people from large corporations said they had training programs in sales, transportation and factory management. They all said there was a great opportunity with their companies. A local department store manager and supermarket manager also showed us how well we could do with them. They talked about opportunities within the several departments in their stores.

With all the choices and opportunities it will be hard to make a decision; but I did appreciate the opportunity to listen to what they all had to say.

Assignment: Rewrite this material in *one paragraph*, using a better selection of words. Eliminate those words or phrases you crossed out. Substitute more precise words for those you underlined.

_____
_____
_____
_____
_____
_____
_____
_____
_____
_____
_____
_____
_____

Name _____

Date _____

REPORT WRITING: BIOGRAPHY I

Directions: The following notes on the life and times of Martin Luther King, Jr., were taken from three different sources. First, eliminate any information that is repeated, unimportant, or unrelated to the topic. Then organize the information according to subtopic and details.

SOURCE A

- early life victim of racial prejudice
- father Baptist minister
- protested segregated buses, restaurants, other public places
- became president of Southern Christian Leadership Conference in 1958
- noted for quote "I have a dream"
- remembered today as champion of civil rights
- writings include "Why We Can't Wait" (1964)
- family not permitted to go anywhere or do anything without discrimination

SOURCE B

- mother was a school teacher
- best noted for attacks on war, poverty
- born on January 15, 1929, in Atlanta, Georgia
- condemned Vietnam Conflict—too many dollars spent, violence
- his death had lasting effect on U.S.
- awarded Nobel Peace Prize (1964)
- an eloquent and forceful speaker
- was very popular in school
- killed by assassin's bullet in Memphis, Tennessee (1968)

SOURCE C

- met wife Coretta in Boston (1953)
- entered Morehouse College at age 15
- believed nonviolent resistance
- rioting by blacks in several U.S. cities following assassination
- birthday commemorated by millions of Americans every year
- at six years of age two white friends not allowed to play with him anymore

Assignment: Organize the notes from the three sources. Would you organize them according to sequence, compare/contrast, or cause/effect? Eliminate any information that is repeated, unimportant, or not related to the other subtopics. Then write this biographical report for your English teacher.

RW 33

Name _____

Date _____

REPORT WRITING: BIOGRAPHY II

Directions: Below are three boxes in which you are to write notes from three different sources dealing with the life of John F. Kennedy. Above each box, write the source of the information, such as an encyclopedia, *Who's Who?*, an old magazine article, or a biography.

When you have finished taking notes, eliminate any information that is repeated, unnecessary, or unrelated to the topic. Then organize the notes by subtopic and details. Finally, write the report for your social studies class.

SOURCE A: _____

SOURCE B: _____

SOURCE C: _____

RW 34

Name _____

Date _____

REPORT WRITING: BIOGRAPHY III

Directions: Below are three boxes in which you are to write notes from three different sources dealing with the life of Susan B. Anthony. Above each box, write the source of the information, such as an encyclopedia, *Who's Who?*, or a biography.

When you have finished taking notes, eliminate any information that is repeated, unnecessary, or unrelated to the topic. Then organize the notes by subtopic and details. Finally, write the report for your social studies class.

SOURCE A: _____

SOURCE B: _____

SOURCE C: _____

Name _____

Date _____

REPORT WRITING: PRACTICE AND REVIEW I

Directions: Write a report using the situation and notes given below.

Situation: You have taken the following notes from different sources for a report on "Species and Varieties of the Cat Family." This written report will be given to your science teacher.

Notes

- several species and varieties of cats in world
- includes wild species plus 30 breeds small domestic cats
- spotted leopard commonly found in East Asia
- known to be 2–2½' long, weigh up to 30 lbs.
- more than 30 million domestic cats living in U.S. alone
- lions found mainly in open plains of Africa
- lion is a meat-eater known to kill zebras and antelopes
- domestic cat one of earliest household pets
- domestic is smallest of cat family—can still be wild and dangerous
- farmers keep cats to control rat and mice populations in barns and houses
- lion known as king of beasts
- grayish-brown in color with many spots on body
- adult lions grow to 300–500 pounds, 6–10' long
- leopard hunts rodents and birds at night; sleeps days

Assignment: Organize these notes according to a plan. Which organizational pattern will you use?

_____

Be sure to include all of the information in your report. Revise your notes before writing your final draft.

RW 36

Name _____

Date _____

REPORT WRITING: PRACTICE AND REVIEW II

Directions: Write a report using the situation and notes given below.

Situation: You were present at a lecture by Dr. Richard Cole, entitled "Running—The Total Exercise." You took the following notes and intend to use them for writing an article for the school newspaper.

Notes

- there are several physical benefits from running
- many Americans unable to complete easy physical tests
- feelings of depression disappear
- produces a more cheerful outlook on life
- helps body tolerate stress and strain
- a real need for more exercise in America
- will definitely increase energy level
- most Americans devote little time to any activity
- benefits skeletal muscles, the heart and lungs
- the mental benefits are truly amazing
- reduces one's desire for alcohol, tobacco, and food
- many different kinds of exercise, running best
- excellent for both men and women

Assignment: Organize these notes according to a plan. Which organizational pattern will you use?

_____

Be sure to include all of the information in your report. Revise your notes before writing your final draft.

Name _____

Date _____

REPORT WRITING: PRACTICE AND REVIEW III

Directions: Write a report using the situation and notes given below.

Situation: In social studies class you are studying the major religions of the world. You have been asked to research three of the most popular religions. The information you find will be reported to the class and will be compared with information on other religions that have been researched by others in the class. Your notes are listed below.

Notes

> Hinduism has no single leader or person to follow
>
> Buddhism is great oriental religion founded by Gautama Buddha
>
> Muslims believe in just one God, Allah, and study bible called Koran
>
> followers of Islam known as Mohammedans or Muslims
>
> Hinduism one of world's great religions—more than 400 million followers
>
> are several religions popular in world
>
> believed to be 550-600 million Buddhists in world
>
> they follow teachings of Mohammed much as Christians follow teachings of Christ
>
> Buddhism started in India, but today most popular in China, Japan, and Southeast Asia
>
> most Hindus live in India
>
> Islam is religion of over 500 million Arabs from Africa, Asia, and Middle East
>
> serve, respect, and idolize their God, Buddha
>
> hundreds of gods, common to every Indian household

Assignment: Organize these notes according to a plan. Which organizational pattern will you use?

_____

Be sure to include all of the information in your report. Revise your notes before writing your final draft.

Name _____

Date _____

REPORT WRITING: PRACTICE AND REVIEW IV

Directions: Write a report using the situation and notes given below.

Situation: As part of an English class assignment, you are to write a report on a favorite hobby or interest. Your notes about gardening are listed below.

Notes

> plant seeds
>
> be sure vegetables are ripe before harvesting
>
> watch out for pests that kill and eat plants
>
> before planting seeds, prepare soil and line up rows
>
> planning the garden begins in February
>
> read seed packets to see best time to plant; mark calendar
>
> don't plant seeds too shallow or deep
>
> if planned and cared for will yield fine crop of fresh produce
>
> must measure and plot garden space
>
> decide what to plant and order through catalog company
>
> tamp down soil gently on top seeds and water
>
> when plants are young, cultivate to keep weeds out

Assignment: Organize these notes according to a plan. Which organizational pattern will you use?

_____

Be sure to include all of the information in your report. Revise your notes before writing your final draft.

RW 39

Name _____

Date _____

REPORT WRITING: PRACTICE AND REVIEW V

Directions: Write a report using the situation and notes given below.

Situation: You have been asked to prepare a report for your science/health teacher on various oils and their uses. Below are the notes you took from several different sources.

Notes

- most animal oils or fats not consumed
- soybean oil single most important oil product in world
- corn oil used to make mayonnaise and salad dressings
- various kinds of oils found in nature
- marine or water-type oils not normally used for eating
- lard a major animal oil—comes from hogs
- oil from whale's blubber for cosmetics, some drugs
- tallows and greases are fats from hogs
- more than ten different kinds of vegetable oils
- most fish oils used in paint products, lubricating greases
- peanut oil second largest eaten worldwide
- after cream separated from cow's raw milk we get butterfat

Assignment: Organize these notes according to a plan. Which organizational pattern will you use?

_____

Be sure to include all of the information in your report. Revise your notes before writing your final draft.

RW 40

REPORT WRITING: OUTLINE FORM

Topic _____ Audience _____

Type of organization _____
(sequence, compare/contrast, cause/effect)

Introduction _____
_____
_____

Suptopic #1 _____
_____

Details about #1 _____
_____
_____
_____

Subtopic #2 _____
_____

Details about #2 _____
_____
_____
_____

Subtopic #3 _____
_____

Details about #3 _____
_____
_____
_____

Conclusion _____
_____
_____
_____

RW 41

REPORT WRITING TOPICS

Classroom or School Activities
curricula
extracurricular activities
rules and policies
athletics
assemblies
homework

cafeteria
any department
favorite subject
worst subject
issues or problems
testing

Individual Interests
family
hobbies
sports
pets
music and art

part-time job
parents' occupations
television or radio programs
neighborhood
books or magazines

Past Experiences
visit to historical attraction or national monument
feelings about something
movie seen in or out of school
most embarrassing, humorous, frightening, or disappointing experience
an earlier teacher or friend

Content Area Subjects
Use specialized vocabulary in sentences or paragraphs.
Summarize a topic, chapter, or unit.
Explain a cause and effect relationship.
Write topic sentences and related paragraphs about randomly organized details.
Write to someone outside of school for more detailed information.
Support or reject statements made in subject area.

Literature
Describe setting.
Describe character appearance.
Describe character behavior.

Compare and contrast two characters.
Summarize plot.

Current Events
energy
conservation
education
taxation
drug abuse
national/international conflicts

government action or inaction
government services
strikes
the draft
court cases

REPORT WRITING: SIGNAL WORDS

Sequence

first	after
next	before
finally	until
last	thereafter
then	immediately
when	simultaneously
while	subsequently
as soon as	at that time
during	

Cause and Effect

since	thus
due to	so
because	if—then
because of	caused by
consequently	as a result
therefore	for this reason

Compare and Contrast

similarly	contrasted with
compared to	likewise
in like manner	in contrast
in the same way	on the contrary
on the other hand	

Conclusion

in conclusion	to sum up
in summary	consequently
as you can see	therefore
finally	the information given above
in short	

LETTER WRITING SKILLS AND ACTIVITIES

Organizing for Letter Writing	LW 1
Audience I	LW 2
Audience II	LW 3
Informal Note	LW 4
Friendly Letter	LW 5
Business Letter: Form	LW 6
Business Letter: Request I	LW 7
Business Letter: Request II	LW 8
Business Letter: Problem and Solution I	LW 9
Business Letter: Problem and Solution II	LW 10
Business Letter: Complaint I	LW 11
Business Letter: Complaint II	LW 12
Business Letter: Cover Letter I	LW 13
Business Letter: Cover Letter II	LW 14
Revising I: Form and Mechanics	LW 15
Revising II: Message	LW 16
Practice and Review I	LW 17
Practice and Review II	LW 18
Practice and Review III	LW 19
Practice and Review IV	LW 20
Practice and Review V	LW 21
Practice and Review VI	LW 22
Letter Writing: Outline Form of Informal and Friendly Letters	LW 23
Letter Writing: Outline Form of Business Letter (Block Form)	LW 24
Letter Writing: Outline Form of Business Letter (Modified Block Form)	LW 25
Letter Writing Topics	LW 26

Name _____

Date _____

ORGANIZING FOR LETTER WRITING

Information: Like all forms of writing, letter writing requires some note taking and organizing prior to the actual rough draft. You must determine the following:

1. Who is the audience?
2. What is the purpose?
3. What do you want to say? What information is necessary to convey that message?

First, jot down your notes. Then organize those notes according to a plan. Finally, write those notes in sentences and paragraphs in a rough draft.

Directions: Read the situation and notes below.

Situation: You have been away from home as a camp counselor for two weeks. Write to your parents and tell them what you are doing and your reactions to the job.

    Audience: Your parents
    Purpose: Tell about job and reactions to it

Notes

Responsibilities—	8 campers in cabin. Help them to get along and to keep cabin clean. Teach beginning and advanced swimming classes all morning. Supervise recreation hall during free time. Help campers work on merit badges in afternoon.
Reactions and feelings—	Thoroughly enjoyable. Have common interests with many new people. Good campers, but have hard time getting along. Youngest one got homesick and left after first week.
At home—	How's family? Any friends call? Be home in two weeks.

Assignment: Write a letter home informing your parents about your work as a camp counselor. Develop three paragraphs using the notes outlined above.

LW 1

Name _____

Date _____

AUDIENCE I

Directions: When you write a letter it makes a difference to whom you are writing. Read these two letters and answer the true/false statements that follow. Be prepared to support your answers.

Dear Mayor Hill:

It has come to my attention that a certain percentage of people living in the West Street area are refusing to cooperate with local regulations. Some are burning their trash and papers daily, even though pollution control laws were passed by the City Council last spring. Others are letting their pets wander throughout the neighborhood. Both these acts are violating local laws. Although there are other laws this group is ignoring, the two mentioned above are most disturbing to me. Your responsibility as the leader of this fine community is to assure that laws are enforced. I would appreciate your helping our neighborhood solve these problems. Thank you, Mayor Hill. I wish you well in the upcoming election.

Sincerely,
Harold Hoarsely

Dear Bruce:

Boy, are you lucky to have moved away from this city last year! Do you remember those three new families living at the other end of West Street? They have been burning their smelly trash every single day now. What they don't manage to burn remains in their yards for the rats and dogs. Speaking of dogs, Old Man Riggins must send his pack of mutts to my yard on purpose. You ought to see the old Johnson place! Those Adams kids have really destroyed it. You would never know those dummies at city hall ever wrote any of those laws dealing with pollution control and leash laws for pets. If Mayor Hill would get off the golf course and out of his swimming pool, he might be able to enforce the laws of this lousy town. He'll never get my vote next November because I'm moving!

Your friend,
Harold Hoarsely

---

1. These letters contain basically the same information. _____
2. There are more than two ways to express your feelings in a letter. _____
3. The letter to Bruce should have been written to the City Council to get better results. _____
4. Harold's letters will probably get a response from both people. _____
5. The letter to Mayor Hill should be changed to make it more convincing. _____

Assignment: You have been selected by your principal to tell the student council your feelings about the school cafeteria food and service. Write one letter to a friend and another to your student council expressing your feelings.

LW 2

Name _____

Date _____

AUDIENCE II

Directions: Read the following audiences and situation.

1. a friend
2. your grandparents
3. the Better Business Bureau
4. a local newspaper

Situation: Your grandparents gave you $125 as a graduation present. You purchased a portable cassette tape recorder that could be used either in your car or at home. The recorder never worked properly, yet the local company, ACE Electronics, failed to fix it or replace it. The salesperson at ACE Electronics remembers selling the unit to you, but refuses to replace it because you do not have a copy of the warranty.

Assignment: Write a letter expressing your feelings to any *two* of the audiences listed above.

LW 3

Name _____

Date _____

INFORMAL NOTE

Information: There are several occasions for writing an informal note. A thank-you, an invitation, or an apology are only a few examples. An informal note is generally written to someone you know quite well, and tends to be short in length and specific in purpose.

The informal note has five basic parts:

1. date
2. salutation
3. body
4. closing
5. signature

Of course the telephone has replaced note-writing in popularity; however, a written message can be very meaningful and lasting, especially when the purpose is to please someone.

Directions: Read the model below and notice its form and brief message.

October 14, 1982

Dear Joanne,

    It's that time of year again! My annual Halloween party is all set for Saturday, October 30, 1982 at 7:30 p.m. at my house. The regular crew from school, as well as a few new friends from work, have all been invited. I'm sure we'll have a great time.

    I don't have to remind you that costumes are required. We are still talking about your munchkin outfit at last year's affair. I can't wait to see your artistic and imaginative getup this year.

    Write back soon with your acceptance. The party wouldn't be the same without you!

                               Yours truly,
                               Brenda

Assignment: Write an informal note to Brenda either accepting or declining her invitation to the Halloween party.

Name _____

Date _____

FRIENDLY LETTER

Information: Similar to informal notes, friendly letters are written to someone you know quite well. The purposes for writing are also varied, but the friendly letter might be more informative and lengthy. There could be several topics to express, especially if you have not seen the person for a while. The form of the friendly letter is also slightly different from an informal note. First, it includes a full heading with your return address and date. Second, the salutation and closing might be very informal and personal, and generally reflect the closeness of the friendship.

Directions: Read the model below and notice its form and style.

> 2427 Taylor Road
> Heights, MT 59288
> November 20, 1982
>
> Hello Big Jim,
>
>   The other day as Phil and I attended the City League Football Championship, I decided it was time to write this long overdue letter.
>   Remember last year when St. Thomas Prep blasted East High 27–0 in that November blizzard? It didn't seem very cold when we were winning! Well, the tables turned this year. Even though the weather was seasonal, it was a cold day for the Saints from Thomas Prep. This year East had control the whole game and won 21–7. There's no doubt the team missed your speed and power at fullback.
>   Since you moved away last summer, there have been a few changes around here. Mr. Hixon, the new principal, seems to be friendly and concerned. He started an intramural sports program so that even uncoordinated klutzes like Phil and me can participate. Not only that, he has encouraged the Student Council and whole school to make suggestions for improvement in school activities. I think it will be a great year.
>   The neighborhood isn't quite the same since you left. The family that bought your house has three kids who are nothing but trouble. The oldest one was caught breaking windows in the Canterbury School last week. The parents don't seem to care where they are or what they do. Oh, well, we'll survive!
>   Write back soon and let us know what's happening.
>
>   The Taylor Road Flash,
>   Richie Levine

Assignment: Write a friendly letter to someone you know whom you have not seen in some time. Follow the form and style of the model shown above. Be sure to mail the letter!

LW 5

Name _____

Date _____

BUSINESS LETTER: FORM

Information: There are two basic forms for business letters: *block form* and *modified block form*. In the block form, the heading, inside address, salutation, body, closing, and signature begin at the left margin of the paper. In the modified block form, the heading, closing, and signature begin at the right of center and do not extend beyond the right margin. The first word in each paragraph in the modified block form is indented. Always use plain white paper for business letters whether you hand-write or type them. Be sure to make your letters brief and to the point.

Directions: Read the two models below. On the line above each one, write whether the model is in block form or in modified block form.

Model 1 _____

                                        2781 Marathon Road
                                        Rochester, MA 01989
                                        November 1, 1982

Station Manager
WBZ Radio
Livingston, MA 01997

Dear Station Manager:

_____
_____
_____
_____

                                        Sincerely,
                                        Bill Nee

Model 2 _____

2781 Marathon Road
Rochester, MA 01989
November 1, 1982

Station Manager
WBZ Radio
Livingston, MA 01997

Dear Station Manager:

_____
_____
_____
_____

Sincerely,
Bill Nee

Assignment: Using one of the model forms shown above, write a letter to the station manager requesting a copy of the October 30, 1982 political editorial entitled, "The Middle East: Beginning and End of Civilization." You plan to enclose 75 cents for postage and handling.

Name _____

Date _____

BUSINESS LETTER: REQUEST I

Information: One purpose for writing letters is to request something from your audience. You might want to order a catalog, buy tickets to a concert, or receive more information about an advertised product. Whatever the purpose, you must remember to use proper form, proofread for any mechanical errors, and give your audience all the information they need to respond to your request.

Directions: Read the model request letter below and answer the questions that follow.

---

472 High Avenue
Columbia, GA 31700

Columbia Modular Homes
1119 East Avenue
Columbia, GA 31700

Dear Sir or Madam:

    I noticed your modular home brochure at the Home and Garden Show last weekend at the Civic Center. There was not much specific information in those brochures. Therefore, I would like you to either mail me more detailed construction specifications or notify one of your representatives to contact me in person.

                                    Sincerely,
                                    Edward Steitler

---

1. Who is the audience? _____

2. What is the purpose for writing? _____
_____
_____

3. Has the writer given all the information necessary for the audience to respond? If not, what else is needed?
_____
_____

4. Has this person used acceptable business letter form? _____

5. Are there any mechanical errors? _____ If so, what are they?
_____
_____
_____

LW 7

Name _____

Date _____

BUSINESS LETTER: REQUEST II

Directions: Read the situation and complete the assignment below.

Situation: You saw the following advertisement in a magazine. You want to see their catalog so that you can order some tapes and records.

BUYING TAPES AND RECORD ALBUMS?

discount prices—25% savings

We have all your favorite rock or
country stars' recordings!
Send for our free catalog

YOU WON'T BELIEVE OUR PRICES!

Acme Sound Shop   11802 Hooper Avenue
Bridgeton, Texas 75588

Assignment: Write a business letter to the Acme Sound Shop. When writing this letter, be sure to:

1. Use an acceptable business letter form.
2. Give complete and accurate information so that the store can respond.
3. Proofread for any mechanical errors.

Name _____

Date _____

BUSINESS LETTER: PROBLEM AND SOLUTION I

Information: Occasionally a problem develops and you must attempt to solve that problem by writing a business letter to the audience. Perhaps you have ordered a product that arrived damaged or requested some information that you never received. In any case, you must fully explain the situation and explain what the audience should do to solve the problem. Make sure you are polite when writing; the problem may only be an honest error.

Directions: Read the model below and answer the questions that follow.

May 7, 1983

12 Church Street
Ogden, MN

Manager
Newbury Springs Campground
Newbury, WV

Dear Manager:

    On April 5, 1983, I sent you a letter requesting campsite reservations for August 15–17. I also enclosed a check for $20 to reserve a camper site. Did you get them? To date, I have not received confirmation of those reservations. Since my vacation is tightly scheduled, I hope you will respond as quickly as possible. If I don't hear from you within ten days, I will be forced to make alternative plans.

                              Sincerely,
                              Bernice Cobbett

---

1. Who is the audience? _____

2. What is the problem? _____
_____

3. What is the writer's solution? _____
_____

4. Has all the necessary information been given in the letter? _____ If not, what else is needed? _____
_____
_____

5. List any problems with form or mechanics. _____
_____
_____

LW 9

Name _____

Date _____

BUSINESS LETTER: PROBLEM AND SOLUTION II

Directions: Read the situation.

Situation: Your school drama club ordered 25 T-shirts with the words "See you in Camelot" printed on each. These shirts will be worn by club members to advertise an upcoming play. You mailed the Orleans Outlet Store a check for $123.75 ($4.95 per shirt) to cover the order. However, only 15 shirts were received. As president of the club, you want to write to the company at Route 488, Orleans, New York 13700.

Assignment: Write a business letter to the Orleans Outlet Store to solve the problem. When writing this letter, be sure to:

1. Use acceptable business letter form.
2. Give complete and accurate information.
3. Solve the problem.
4. Proofread for mechanical errors.

LW 10

Name _____

Date _____

BUSINESS LETTER: COMPLAINT I

Information: This type of business letter is used after you have made every attempt to solve the problem. Like the problem/solution letter, the tone of your letter should be polite. However, your solution is more forceful and direct.

Your audience most likely has been "To whom it may concern" or "Sir or Madam." The complaint letter should now be directed to someone in charge, perhaps the Manager or the President. Remember, your primary purpose is still to solve the problem. Therefore, it is important to carefully explain the situation forcefully and politely.

Directions: Read the model complaint letter below and answer the questions that follow.

---

21 Green Street
Graham, NH 03599
September 27, 1982

Mayor Edwin Riley
Municipal Building
Centerville, NH 03928

Dear Mayor Riley:

    I have tried, without success, on three occasions to correct an obvious error of mistaken identity. On June 12, 1982 I received a bill in the amount of $10 for a parking violation in your city on May 30, 1982. I attempted to explain, first by telephone and later in two letters, to the Police Department that I was not in Centerville on that date. In fact, I was in Boston visiting relatives over the Memorial Day holiday. Yesterday, I received another bill for $10 plus a $5 late fee. An attached letter threatened to notify the Department of Motor Vehicles of the delinquency so that I could not renew my license.
    I resent this whole situation! What additional action do I have to take to resolve this error? I have contacted my lawyer and will request a lawsuit if <u>you</u> do not do something immediately. It is apparent your Police Department cannot handle it.

                                  Respectfully,
                                  John W. Smith

---

1. Has Mr. Smith attempted to solve the problem? _____

2. Is the information clearly stated? _____ If not, what else is needed?

_____

3. How does Mr. Smith still attempt to solve the problem? _____

_____

4. How might you have written this complaint differently? _____

_____

LW 11

Name _____

Date _____

BUSINESS LETTER: COMPLAINT II

Directions: Read the situation.

Situation: The Treadwell Tire Company on Park Avenue in Milton, Arkansas sold you four new radial tires that were guaranted for 40,000 miles. One of the front tires blew out five months after your purchase. As a result of the blowout, you lost control of the car, hit a pothole, and broke the left front shock and spring. You want the tire, shock, and spring replaced free of charge since the tire was defective. The local manager refused to cooperate. He said you cannot prove the tire was defective.

Assignment: Write to the President of Treadwell Tire Company in Fair Ridge, Ohio 45289 concerning this situation. Be sure to:

1. Explain the situation completely and accurately.
2. Complain politely and offer your solution.
3. Use acceptable business letter form.
4. Proofread for mechanical errors.

LW 12

Name _____

Date _____

BUSINESS LETTER: COVER LETTER I

Information: When you apply for a job or when you are sending important information to someone, a cover letter should be attached to the application or the information. Use an acceptable business letter form and give the audience a brief summary of why you are writing and what you have attached. If the cover letter accompanies a job application or résumé, be sure to highlight your strengths and specific skills.

Directions: Read the model cover letter below and answer the questions that follow.

---

28 South Street
Danbury, SC 29598
January 18, 1983

Personnel Manager
Smithson, Inc.
Route 7
Ventnor, SC 29391

Dear Personnel Manager:

    I noticed with interest your advertisement for an assistant welder in last Sunday's paper. I have attached a résumé for your information, hoping you will send me an application. I am available for an interview any time.
    Please note that I recently graduated from Middle Valley Vocational and Technical School, where I successfully completed two years of welding classes. I have also worked for Wilkerson Welding for the past two years.
    I look forward to hearing from you. You may call me at home at 442-8968.

                        Sincerely,
                        Wilfred Williams

---

1. Does the cover letter explain why Wilfred Williams is writing? _____
2. What two things does the writer want as a result of his writing this letter?

_____

_____

_____

3. Does the writer list any specific skills he has learned? _____
   Should he? _____ Why or why not? _____

_____

4. Is there any other information he should have included in the cover letter? _____ If so, what? _____

_____

5. Would you, as personnel manager, grant the writer an interview? Why or why not? _____

_____

LW 13

Name _____

Date _____

BUSINESS LETTER: COVER LETTER II

Directions: Read the situation.

Situation: The following advertisement appeared in your local paper's Sunday edition. You want to receive an application and be given an interview. You plan to attach a résumé with your request. (For the purposes of this assignment, make up any information necessary to complete the letter and résumé.)

> Assistant Manager Trainee. Ambitious person with pleasant personality needed. Restaurant experience helpful but not necessary. Apply to Manager, Red Rooster Restaurants, 1204 Monroe Avenue, Albany, Alabama 35373.

Assignment: Write a cover letter to the manager. When writing this letter, be sure to:

1. Use acceptable business letter form.
2. Explain why you are writing.
3. Highlight your interests, experiences, and background.
4. Proofread for any mechanical errors.

LW 14

REVISING I: FORM AND MECHANICS

Information: There are several forms of letter writing, and the one you use depends upon the type of letter and its purpose. Whether you are writing an informal note, a friendly letter, or a business letter, make sure the form suits the purpose.

The mechanics of a letter, such as spelling, punctuation, capitalization, and grammar, must be accurate. Otherwise, your intended audience will be distracted and the message may lose its importance.

Directions: Read the situation and letter below and underline any problems in form or mechanics.

Situation: A letter has been written to the principal of an elementary school in hopes of getting a job as a teacher's aide in the summer school program.

Howard Forbs, Principal
Kennedy elementary school
Homesdale CA, 95332

Dear Mr. Forbs,

    I have recently completed High School and will be entering Hillside community college in in September. I understand there are several opening in the Kennedy school for teachers aides this summer. I would like to be considered. For this position because I enjoy working with kids and I may even want to teach someday.

I have worked with kids at the lakemont community center and at a day camp. I hope you will consider me for the job.

                                            Sincerely
                                            Frank Lisi

Assignment: Identify the problems with form and mechanics in this letter. Then rewrite the letter after revising the mistakes.

Name _____
Date _____

REVISING II: MESSAGE

Information: Form and mechanics are certainly important aspects of all letter writing. But if the message is not clearly understood by your audience, they will not likely respond as you intend. There are two things you can do to make your message clear. First, organize your ideas by topic *before* writing the rough draft. Second, let a friend, classmate, or family member read the rough draft.

Directions: Read the situation and model letter below. Then answer the questions that follow.

Situation: You went to a restaurant recently with two out-of-state friends who were visiting for a few days. You had to wait an unreasonable amount of time to be served, the meal was cold, and the waiter was rude. The delay caused you to be late to a concert and you were thoroughly embarrassed. Express your feelings to the manager.

21990 Center Road
Solitude, VT 05203
September 15, 1982

Manager
Dressler's Restaurant
Solitude, VT 05203

Dear Manager:

    Two out-of-state friends were visiting me last week and I wanted to treat them to a special dinner at Dressler's Restaurant. I heard from several people that Dressler's food and service are the best in the area. After my experience, I would never recommend your establishment to anybody! My friends are from New Orleans, a city with great restaurants, and I wanted to show off Northern cooking. Boy was I embarrassed.
    I don't know who is at fault, but I would urge you to take a close look at the whole operation at Dressler's. If you don't correct these problems, you won't be in business much longer.

                                               Sincerely,
                                               Madge Harper

---

1. Does the manager know how the writer feels? _____

2. Does the writer specifically state what the problems are? _____

   What has she failed to say? _____

_____

3. How would you, as manager, react or respond to this letter? _____

_____

Assignment: Rewrite this letter, clearly and specifically expressing your message to the manager.

Name _____

Date _____

PRACTICE AND REVIEW I

Directions: Read the situation and determine the audience, purpose, and type of letter (informal, friendly, business) to write.

Situation: Your wealthy uncle is a businessman who lives in London, England. He mailed you the perfect birthday gift. (The gift is whatever you want it to be.) Although it arrived late and the package was slightly damaged, your gift was not harmed. His address is: 4 Garden Estates, London.

Audience: _____

Purpose: _____

Type of letter: _____

Assignment: Write to your uncle to thank him for his generosity and thoughtfulness. When writing this letter, be sure to:

1. Use an acceptable form.
2. Make your message clear.
3. Revise any mechanical errors in spelling, capitalization, punctuation, sentence structure, etc.

Name _____

Date _____

PRACTICE AND REVIEW II

Directions: Read the situation and determine the audience, purpose, and type of letter (informal, friendly, business) to write.

Situation: You recently read a book, *The Challengers,* by Diane Pettibone Fox. Because it was the best historical novel you have ever read, you decided to inquire about three other novels she wrote. The local librarian gave you the address of the publishing company: Coronet Publishers, Inc., 205 Sylvia Avenue, Western City, Florida 31621.

Audience: _____

Purpose: _____

Type of letter: _____

Assignment: Write to the publishing company to ask for information and an order form so that you can purchase the author's other three novels. When writing this letter, be sure to:

1. Use an acceptable form.
2. Make your message clear.
3. Revise any mechanical errors in spelling, capitalization, punctuation, sentence structure, etc.

LW 18

Name _____

Date _____

PRACTICE AND REVIEW III

Directions: Read the situation and determine the audience, purpose, and type of letter (informal, friendly, business) to write.

Situation: A classified ad for an office secretary told you to apply in person to Henderson Electronics, Old State Road, Clifton, Kentucky 41508. Because there were so many applicants, the Assistant Personnel Manager, Mrs. Eleanor Howell, gave everyone an application. She asked you to return it with a cover letter within five days.

Audience: _____

Purpose: _____

Type of letter: _____

Assignment: Write a cover letter to be sent along with your application. When writing this letter, be sure to:

1. Use an acceptable form.
2. Make your message clear.
3. Revise any mechanical errors in spelling, capitalization, punctuation, sentence structure, etc.

LW 19

Name _____

Date _____

PRACTICE AND REVIEW IV

Directions: Read the situation and determine the audience, purpose, and type of letter (informal, friendly, business) to write.

Situation: You signed an agreement with R.V.A. Record Club (P.O. Box 9701, New York, New York 10200) to buy eight records or tapes at $7.95 each within one year. The contract stated that you did *not* have to accept their monthly selections; it was possible to buy from the catalog at any time. However, R.V.A. has been billing you $7.95 plus $.75 postage and handling for the past three months. As yet, you have not selected any records or tapes.

Audience: _____

Purpose: _____

Type of letter: _____

Assignment: Write to the record club to solve the problem. When writing this letter, be sure to:

1. Use an acceptable form.
2. Make your message clear.
3. Revise any mechanical errors in spelling, capitalization, punctuation, sentence structure, etc.

LW 20

Name _____

Date _____

PRACTICE AND REVIEW V

Directions: Read the situation and determine the audience, purpose, and type of letter (informal, friendly, business) to write.

Situation: You live in Mountainside Apartments complex owned by J.L. Rentals, Inc., of Bingham, Colorado 80608. The superintendent of that complex has been careless in his duties and rude in dealing with the tenants. Among other things, he has failed to repair plumbing and electrical problems, has neglected to keep the grounds attractive and litter-free, and has used profanity repeatedly in dealing with renters.

Audience: _____

Purpose: _____

Type of letter: _____

Assignment: Write to the owners to inform them of this situation. When writing this letter, be sure to:

1. Use an acceptable form.
2. Make your message clear.
3. Revise any mechanical errors in spelling, capitalization, punctuation, sentence structure, etc.

LW 21

Name_____

Date _____

PRACTICE AND REVIEW VI

Directions: Read the situation and determine the audience, purpose, and type of letter (informal, friendly, business) to write.

Situation: Your closest friend went to a college that is more than 1,200 miles from home. Therefore, you have not seen him or her since early September and will not likely get together until Christmas vacation.

Audience: _____

Purpose: _____

Type of letter: _____

Assignment: Write a letter to your friend bringing him or her up to date on all the latest school, family, and social news. When writing this letter, be sure to:

1. Use an acceptable form.
2. Make your message clear.
3. Revise any mechanical errors in spelling, capitalization, punctuation, sentence structure, etc.

LETTER WRITING: OUTLINE FORM OF INFORMAL AND FRIENDLY LETTERS

Heading
(Informal—date only)

Salutation

Body

Closing

Signature

LETTER WRITING: OUTLINE FORM OF BUSINESS LETTER (BLOCK FORM)

Heading

Inside address

Salutation

Body

Closing

Signature

LETTER WRITING: OUTLINE FORM OF BUSINESS LETTER (MODIFIED BLOCK FORM)

- Heading
- Inside address
- Salutation
- Body
- Closing
- Signature

LETTER WRITING TOPICS

Write a letter to: a friend
a family member
your congressman
your principal
your mayor
a local merchant
the police department
a local museum
the newspaper

About:
a trip you took
a graduation gift sent to you
a new proposed law
a way to improve the school
the need for a traffic light at a dangerous intersection
a poor product
heroic actions while apprehending a robber
information you need for a history project
the comments of a politician